ACHIEVING YOUR FULL POTENTIAL

ACHIEVING YOUR FULL POTENTIAL

# ACHIEVING YOUR FULL POTENTIAL

## A Multi-Dimensional Approach to Flourishing in Your Career and at Work

Jonathan H. Westover, PhD

# ACHIEVING YOUR FULL POTENTIAL

Copyright © 2024 Jonathan H. Westover

All rights reserved. This book or parts thereof may not be reproduced in any form, stored in any retrieval system, or transmitted in any form by any means—electronic, mechanical, photocopy, recording, or otherwise—without prior written permission of the publisher, except as provided by United States of America copyright law. For permission requests, write to the author, at "Attention: Permissions Coordinator," at jon.westover@gmail.com.

Achieving Your Full Potential: A Multi-Dimensional Approach to Flourishing in Your Career and at Work / Jonathan H. Westover, author.

ISBN-13: 979-834346-832-8 (HCI Press)

Key Terms: 1. Potential. 2. Achievement 3. Human Flourishing 4. Work I. Westover, Jonathan H.

First published/printed in 2024 in the USA.

Published by HCI Press,

an imprint of Human Capital Innovations, LLC.

www.innovativehumancapital.com

# ACHIEVING YOUR FULL POTENTIAL

ACHIEVING YOUR FULL POTENTIAL

# TABLE OF CONTENTS

**Preface** .............................. xix

**Chapter 1:** Unlocking Your Highest Contribution: A Holistic Approach to Success in Your Career and at Work . . . 1

## Part 1: Work-life Balance and Well-Being

**Chapter 2:** Beyond the Myth of the All-Consuming Work Style: The Path to Work-Life Balance for Leaders . . . . 11

**Chapter 3:** What Research Says about the Dangers of Long Working Hours .......................... 17

**Chapter 4:** Taking Control of Burnout: Shifting from Victim to Empowered .......................... 27

**Chapter 5:** From Languishing to Flourishing: 3 Steps to Find Meaning in Your Career .......................... 33

## Part 2: Early Career Development

**Chapter 6:** Growing Your Career in a Virtual World: Tips for Young Workers .......................... 43

**Chapter 7:** Taking Control of Your Onboarding: A Guide to Success in Your New Job .................. 51

**Chapter 8:** Navigating the Workplace: Strategies for Advancing Your Career .................. 57

**Chapter 9:** Unlocking the Power of Personal Motivation: Strategies for Success When You Just Don't Want To    63

**Chapter 10:** Overcoming Imposter Syndrome: Building Confidence in Your Career ................... 71

## Part 3: Career Navigation and Improvement

**Chapter 11:** Breaking Free from a Toxic Work Environment: Strategies for Leaving a Bad Job ................. 79

**Chapter 12:** The Myth of 100% Motivation: Why You're Probably Under-Performing at Work and How to Fix It    85

**Chapter 13:** Making Better Career Decisions: A 5-Step Framework ....................... 99

**Chapter 14:** The Power of Serendipity in Your Career: How to Cultivate Luck and Success ................. 105

## Part 4: Expanding Your Career Impact

**Chapter 15:** Building Relationships: The Key to Unlocking Career Advancement ....................... 115

**Chapter 16:** Millennial Managers: Driving Positive Change in the Workplace .......................... 121

**Chapter 17:** Finding Your Voice: Speaking Up When It Matters .......................... 127

**Chapter 18:** Developing Your Influence Skills: How to Effectively Persuade Others and Promote Your Ideas.. 133

**Chapter 19:** The Dangers of Workplace Enmeshment: How a Career Can Consume Your Identity and What to Do About It .................... 141


## Part 5: Change Management and Adaptability

**Chapter 20:** Adapting to Change: The Four Attributes of Successful Learners .................... 153

**Chapter 21:** Change Management: Navigating the Turbulent Waters of Organizational Change ............ 159

**Chapter 22:** The Power of "How": Transforming Our Approach to Problem-Solving .................... 167

**Chapter 23:** The Performance Management Revolution: Moving Away from Traditional Appraisals ..... 173

**Chapter 24:** Empowering Employees to Go Beyond Their Jobs: The Art of Citizenship Crafting ............ 179

## Part 6: Personal Leadership Development

**Chapter 25**: The Power of Untouchable Days: Protecting Your Creative Flow ......................... 189

**Chapter 26**: The Art of Letting Go: Shifting from Ego-Drive to Co-Drive Leadership .......................... 197

**Chapter 27**: The Power of Soft Skills: Unlocking Success in the Workplace ......................... 205

**Chapter 28**: Investing in Self-Awareness and Accountability: Mastering Foundational Capabilities for Team Success. . 211

**Chapter 29:** Striking the Balance: Sharing Your Authentic Self at Work ................................. 217

**Chapter 30:** The Art of Building Trust: Strategies for Managing a Colleague Who Doesn't Like You ..... 223

**Chapter 31:** The Challenge of Working with Colleagues Who Aren't Self-Aware ......................... 229


## Part 7: Leading Teams and Organizations

**Chapter 32:** Overcoming the Tyranny of the Urgent: Prioritizing What Really Matters ................... 241

**Chapter 33:** The Importance of Balancing Task- and People-Focus in Leadership .......................... 247

**Chapter 34:** Building and Maintaining Organizational Trust: Avoidable Pitfalls and Proven Strategies ........... 253

**Chapter 35:** The Neuroscience of Trust: How Managers Can Boost Engagement ........................ 263

## Part 8: Effectiveness and Productivity

**Chapter 36:** Overcoming the Tyranny of the Urgent: Prioritizing What Really Matters ........... 275

**Chapter 37:** Ways to Better Understand Your Emotions 281

**Chapter 38:** Giving Effective Feedback When You're Short on Time ............................... 287

**Chapter 39:** Building Stronger Relationships at Work: The Power of Effective Listening .................. 293

**Chapter 40:** Unlocking Meaning and Purpose at Work: The Power of Curiosity ........................ 299

**Chapter 41:** The Myth of Hard Work: Why Intelligence and Direction Matter as Much as Effort . . . . . . . . . . . 305

## Part 9: Your Journey Continues

**Chapter 42:** Reflections on the Path Ahead: Maintaining Momentum Towards Your Vision . . . . . . . . . . . 315

About the Author . . . . . . . . . . . . . . . . . . . . . . . . 321

# ACHIEVING YOUR FULL POTENTIAL

ACHIEVING YOUR FULL POTENTIAL

# ACKNOWLEDGMENTS

First and foremost, I would like to publicly thank my wife (Jacque) and my six wonderful children (Sara, Amber, Lia, Kaylie, David, and Brayden) for all their love and support! I would also like to thank my many colleagues who have worked with me over the years. Each has helped to inform and refine my thinking and worldview, as well as my leadership practice. I would also like to thank all the researchers and practitioners that have come before me. I am just adding a brick to the wall of academic and practical knowledge that you have all built!

# ACHIEVING YOUR FULL POTENTIAL

# ACHIEVING YOUR FULL POTENTIAL

# ACHIEVING YOUR FULL POTENTIAL

## PREFACE

We live in a world where achieving success in our careers and maximizing our potential at work is increasingly important, yet also increasingly challenging. Constant change, disruptive technologies, and a blurring of work-life boundaries have complicated the path forward.

This book aims to provide a comprehensive yet practical guide for flourishing in your career and achieving your full potential at work. Based on the latest research and real-world experiences, it offers a holistic, multidimensional framework and specific actionable strategies across nine key domains: work-life balance and well-being, early career development, career navigation and improvement, expanding your career impact, change management and adaptability, personal leadership development, leading teams and organizations, effectiveness and productivity, and planning for your ongoing journey.

Within each domain, you will find chapters addressing topics like managing burnout, navigating organizational change, overcoming imposter syndrome, developing soft skills, empowering others, and more. Whether you are just starting your career, looking to advance, or aiming to lead high-performing teams, this book provides a roadmap to help you unlock your highest contribution and maximize your success at every stage.

Rooted in positivity and empowerment, this book is about taking control of your career and work experience. It will help you shift from being a victim of external forces to an empowered agent of your own destiny. By sharing both research and real-world examples, it brings theory and practice together in an accessible yet thought-provoking way.

**Structure of the Book**

This book provides a comprehensive yet practical guide to achieving your full potential and flourishing in your career and at work.

Within these pages, you will discover a holistic, multi-dimensional framework built around nine core domains that impact career success and work satisfaction. Each domain contains focused chapters addressing contemporary challenges and opportunities, grounded in the latest research yet presented in an accessible, engaging style.

The book begins by laying the foundation for success. Part 1 examines critical aspects of work-life balance and well-being, debunking myths around excessive work hours and providing actionable strategies for taking control of burnout.

## ACHIEVING YOUR FULL POTENTIAL

You will learn how to find meaning and purpose to flourish in your career.

Part 2 focuses on the early stages of career development. Whether just entering the workforce or starting a new role, you will discover tips for navigating virtual onboarding processes and overcoming common hurdles like managing motivation and imposter syndrome.

As your career progresses, Part 3 equips you with tools to continually adapt, improve and advance. You will learn frameworks for making better decisions and cultivating serendipity, as well as how to leave toxic environments and overcome underperformance.

Expanding your impact, Part 4 explores relationship building, public speaking, influencing skills and maintaining a healthy professional identity amid change.

Managing change effectively is the focus of Part 5, with chapters addressing adaptability, change leadership, problem-solving, performance management innovations and empowering employees.

Personal leadership skills critical for long-term success, such as protecting creative flow, engaging in co-drive leadership, developing soft abilities and maintaining self-awareness.

Effective team leadership behaviors are at the center of Part 7, coupled with chapters on building organizational trust, managing employees beyond job descriptions with empowered citizenship, and leveraging neuroscientific insights.

Part 8 zooms in on productivity enhancements like prioritization, emotions intelligence, giving feedback, active listening, cultivating curiosity and challenging assumptions about effort.

Finally, Part 9 ties it all together with reflections on maintaining momentum along your career journey and continuously striving to reach new heights.

## Conclusion

My hope is that this multidimensional guide equipped with ample research, examples and exercises serves you well in achieving career fulfilment and unlocking your true potential. The road ahead starts here.

# ACHIEVING YOUR FULL POTENTIAL

# ACHIEVING YOUR FULL POTENTIAL

# ACHIEVING YOUR FULL POTENTIAL

# ACHIEVING YOUR FULL POTENTIAL

# Chapter 1

## Unlocking Your Highest Contribution: A Holistic Approach to Success in Your Career and at Work

Welcome to this guide for achieving your full potential and flourishing in your career. Over the course of the following chapters, we will explore a holistic, multi-dimensional framework to help you navigate various aspects of work life and unlock continuous self-improvement.

But before diving into specific strategies and techniques, it's important to start by gaining clarity on your deeper motivations and vision for success. This foundational chapter is designed to help you articulate your "why"—the true drivers behind your career aspirations, beyond just job titles or salary figures. Grounding yourself in this awareness provides the guiding light to effectively utilize the tactical advice in later parts of the book.

So, let's begin our journey together by reflecting on some fundamental questions: What really matters most to you? How do you authentically define success for your life and work? And how can you craft a vision aligned with your core values, strengths and passions? The answers will form the foundation from which you can strategically work towards your highest potential.

**What Really Matters**

Too often in our fast-paced, results-driven culture, we lose touch with our deeper motivations and get caught up chasing externally defined metrics of achievement. But true fulfilment comes from aligning our efforts with what we find truly meaningful. As a first exercise, take some time on your own to thoughtfully reflect on and journal answers to questions like:

- What are the core values that drive how you show up each day? Values like family, integrity, contribution, creativity, autonomy, etc.
- Beyond career and financial aspirations, what life priorities are most significant - health, spirituality, community impact, personal growth?
- What types of contribution or change do you feel passionately compelled to make through your work - solving important problems, empowering others, spreading positivity?

Clarity on your fundamental values and sense of purpose will become the guiding light and fuel for your work. It helps ensure each step of your career journey enhances who you are and what you hold important, rather than defines you.

**Reimagining Success**

Once clear on your core values and motivators, reflect on how you currently define success. For many, conditioned definitions revolve around career trajectories, competitive comparisons or financial milestones that don't align authentically. It's time to thoughtfully reimagine success based on what truly resonates as meaningful for your life.

## ACHIEVING YOUR FULL POTENTIAL

Some alternative success definitions could include:

- Feeling passionate daily in a role aligned with your strengths
- Maintaining vibrant relationships and a solid work-life integration
- Thriving mental and physical well-being throughout your career
- Making a meaningful impact on an important issue or people
- Continuously growing as a person through challenging experiences

Define success authentically through your lens, not society's or any other external validators. This internal clarity is empowering for ongoing motivation when challenges inevitably emerge.

**Crafting Your Vision**

With values and success recalibrated, you now have a strong foundation to craft a future vision bringing it all together. Envision specifically what you see yourself doing through your strengths to contribute and make a difference. Picture the type of workplace culture and projects that energize you. You may see:

- Yourself as a leader empowering others to solve key problems through innovation
- A dynamic role combining strategy with hands-on project work and travel
- Starting an enterprise combining your passion for the environment and business
- A flexible remote career path leaving more time for family

Be as descriptive as possible to paint a vivid picture of your preferred future state. This vision, grounded in who you are and what you care about, becomes your true north star - an inspiration to guide strategic actions and choices along the way.

**Unlocking Your Potential**

I hope this opening chapter has helped you gain deeper clarity on your intrinsic values and authentic vision of career success beyond superficial definitions. With solid self-awareness of what really drives and fulfills you, you now have an aligned framework and perspective to guide next steps. The following multidimensional action tools can be leveraged strategically to continuously progress towards your highest contribution and true potential. May this journey of ongoing growth and achievement be truly fulfilling for you!

# ACHIEVING YOUR FULL POTENTIAL

# ACHIEVING YOUR FULL POTENTIAL

ACHIEVING YOUR FULL POTENTIAL

# Part 1

# Work-life Balance and Well-Being

# ACHIEVING YOUR FULL POTENTIAL

# Chapter 2

## Beyond the Myth of the All-Consuming Work Style: The Path to Work-Life Balance for Leaders

The mantra of many successful leaders has long been that intense and all-consuming work styles are the only way to reach the top and achieve success. However, a growing group of executives is challenging this notion and finding innovative ways to balance work, family, and life. Over the past 20 years, this group has been meeting and sharing their ideas for cultivating skills that allow them to prioritize work-life balance without sacrificing their professional goals.

In this chapter, we will explore the three key relationships that these leaders have found essential in achieving balance and the stories of three leaders who exemplify this approach.

**Why Leaders Need to Prioritize Their Own Well-Being**

It is essential for leaders to prioritize their own well-being in order to effectively lead their organizations. When leaders prioritize their own well-being, they are better able to maintain their physical, mental, and emotional health, which in turn enables them to perform at their best and lead their organizations to success.

Leaders who prioritize their own well-being set a positive example for their employees, demonstrating that taking care of oneself is important and acceptable. This helps to create a culture where employees feel empowered to prioritize their own well-being, leading to increased job satisfaction, productivity, and employee retention.

Furthermore, when leaders prioritize their own well-being, they are better able to lead by example. They are more focused, present, and able to connect with their employees on a deeper level, which enables them to inspire and motivate their teams more effectively. This leads to a more positive and productive work environment, where employees feel valued and supported.

Prioritizing one's own well-being is not a luxury, but a necessity for effective leadership. By taking care of themselves, leaders are better able to take care of their organizations and lead their employees to success.

## Relationship with Teams at Work

One of the most significant obstacles to work-life balance for leaders is the pressure to be constantly available and responsive to the needs of their teams. However, the executives in this group have found that by working differently with their teams, they can not only reduce their workload but also increase productivity and job satisfaction.

One such leader is Sarah, a CEO of a technology startup. Sarah realized that she was setting a poor example for her team by constantly working long hours and being available 24/7. She decided to implement a "no email Fridays" policy and encouraged her team to take breaks and prioritize their personal time. By doing so, she found that her team was more productive and motivated, and she was able to spend more time with her family.

## Relationship with Family

Another critical relationship that leaders must cultivate is with their families. It can be challenging to put family first when work demands are high, but these executives have found that making a plan with their families is essential to achieving balance.

John, a senior executive at a Fortune 500 company, made a plan with his wife to set aside dedicated time for family activities, such as dinner together and weekend outings. He also established a "no work Sundays" rule, which allowed him to recharge and spend quality time with his family. By prioritizing his family in this way, John found that he was able to be more present and engaged in both his personal and professional life.

## Relationship with Oneself

The third and perhaps most critical relationship that leaders must cultivate is with themselves. It is all too easy to become consumed by work and neglect one's own needs and well-being. However, these executives have found that shifting their mindset and giving themselves permission to prioritize their own needs is essential to achieving balance.

Maria, a founder of a successful startup, found that she was constantly putting her own needs last. She decided to take a step back and prioritize her own well-being by practicing meditation and taking time for self-reflection. By doing so, Maria found that she was able to be more present and focused in her work, and she was able to make better decisions that benefited both her company and her personal life.

## Conclusion

The stories of these leaders show that it is possible to achieve work-life balance without sacrificing professional success. By cultivating skills in three key relationships - with their teams at work, their families, and themselves - leaders can create a more sustainable and fulfilling approach to work and life. It takes courage and commitment to challenge the status quo and prioritize balance, but the results are well worth it. As Sarah, John, and Maria demonstrate, it is possible to be successful leaders who also have fulfilling personal lives. It is possible to break free from the myth of the all-consuming work style and find a better way. By following their example and cultivating skills in these three key relationships, leaders can achieve a more balanced and sustainable approach to work and life that benefits everyone involved.

# ACHIEVING YOUR FULL POTENTIAL

# Chapter 3

## What Research Says about the Dangers of Long Working Hours

In today's fast-paced and competitive business environment, it is not uncommon for employees to work long hours. In fact, many employees take pride in putting in extra time at the office, often sacrificing their personal lives in the process. However, research suggests that working long hours can have negative consequences for both employees and employers.

In this chapter, we will look at what recent research says about the dangers of long working hours for individuals and for organizations.

## Negative Impact on Employee Well-being

Research has shown that working long hours can have a negative impact on employee well-being. Long hours can lead to physical and mental health problems, such as cardiovascular disease, diabetes, and depression. A study published in the Journal of Occupational and Environmental Medicine found that employees who worked more than 11 hours per day were more likely to develop chronic health problems.

One example of a company that has recognized the importance of employee well-being is Google. Google provides its employees with a variety of benefits and perks, such as free meals, on-site fitness classes, and unlimited vacation time. This approach has led to high levels of employee satisfaction and productivity.

## Decreased Productivity

Contrary to popular belief, working long hours does not necessarily lead to increased productivity. In fact, research has shown that working long hours can actually decrease productivity. A study published in the Journal of Applied

Psychology found that employees who worked 60 hours per week were less productive than those who worked 40 hours per week.

One example of a company that has implemented policies to promote productivity is Amazon. Amazon has implemented a policy of "work-life balance" which allows employees to work from home or have flexible work arrangements. This approach has led to increased productivity and employee satisfaction.

## Increased Absenteeism and Turnover

Working long hours can also lead to increased absenteeism and turnover. Employees who are overworked and stressed are more likely to take days off or quit their jobs altogether. A study published in the Journal of Vocational Behavior found that employees who worked long hours were more likely to leave their jobs.

One example of a company that has recognized the importance of work-life balance is Patagonia. Patagonia has implemented a policy of "100% paid time off" for employees to take time off for environmental activism. This approach has led to high levels of employee satisfaction and retention.

## Negative Impact on Companies

Not only do long working hours have negative consequences for employees, but they also have negative consequences for companies. Long hours can lead to increased recruitment and training costs, as well as decreased employee morale and productivity.

A study published in the Journal of Occupational and Organizational Psychology found that companies that promoted work-life balance had higher levels of employee engagement and productivity.

One example of a company that has recognized the importance of work-life balance is The Container Store. The Container Store has implemented a policy of "flexible work arrangements" which allows employees to work from home or have flexible work schedules. This approach has led to high levels of employee satisfaction and productivity.

## What Leaders and Organizations Should Do to Avoid Overwork

There are several steps that leaders and organizations can take to address the issue of long working hours and promote work-life balance for their employees. Here are some proactive steps they can take:

## ACHIEVING YOUR FULL POTENTIAL

1. *Set clear expectations and boundaries*: Leaders can set clear expectations and boundaries around work hours and workload to ensure that employees are not overworked. They can communicate the importance of work-life balance and encourage employees to prioritize their personal well-being.

2. *Provide flexible work arrangements*: Organizations can offer flexible work arrangements such as telecommuting, flexible hours, or job sharing to help employees balance their work and personal responsibilities. This can help reduce the need for long working hours and allow employees to have more control over their schedules.

3. *Encourage employee well-being initiatives*: Leaders can encourage employee well-being initiatives such as mental health support, stress management training, and physical fitness programs. This can help employees manage stress and maintain their physical and mental health.

4. *Monitor workloads*: Leaders can monitor workloads and ensure that employees are not overwhelmed with too much work. They can also provide training and

resources to help employees manage their workload effectively.

5. *Lead by example*: Leaders can model healthy work habits themselves by taking breaks, using vacation time, and prioritizing their own work-life balance. This can help create a culture that values work-life balance and encourages employees to do the same.

6. *Conduct regular check-ins*: Leaders can conduct regular check-ins with employees to discuss their workload, stress levels, and overall well-being. This can help identify potential issues before they become major problems.

7. *Provide employee recognition and rewards*: Organizations can provide recognition and rewards for employees who prioritize work-life balance and take care of their personal well-being. This can help incentivize employees to prioritize their personal health and well-being.

8. *Implement policies to support work-life balance*: Organizations can implement policies such as paid parental leave, flexible work arrangements, and

employee wellness programs to support work-life balance.

9. *Encourage open communication*: Leaders can encourage open communication about work-life balance and create a culture where employees feel comfortable discussing their needs and concerns. This can help identify potential issues and address them before they become major problems.

10. *Monitor progress*: Leaders can monitor progress towards work-life balance and make adjustments as needed. They can track metrics such as employee turnover, absenteeism, and productivity to assess the effectiveness of their efforts.

By taking these proactive steps, leaders and organizations can promote work-life balance for their employees and reduce the negative impact of long working hours. This can lead to increased productivity, employee satisfaction, and retention, as well as improved overall well-being.

## Conclusion

The research is clear that long working hours can have negative consequences for both employees and companies. Long hours can lead to physical and mental health problems, decreased productivity, increased absenteeism and turnover, and negative impacts on companies. Companies that prioritize work-life balance, such as Google, Amazon, Patagonia, and The Container Store, have seen increased employee satisfaction, productivity, and retention. It is time for companies to recognize the importance of work-life balance and implement policies that promote the well-being of their employees.

# ACHIEVING YOUR FULL POTENTIAL

ACHIEVING YOUR FULL POTENTIAL

# Chapter 4

## Taking Control of Burnout: Shifting from Victim to Empowered

Burnout is a state of emotional, mental, and physical exhaustion that can leave individuals feeling powerless and trapped in their circumstances. It's easy to fall into a victim mindset, believing that there's nothing that can be done to change the situation. However, this way of thinking only perpetuates the cycle of burnout and prevents individuals from taking action to improve their situation.

In this chapter, we will explore how shifting from a victim mindset to an empowered one can help individuals take control of their burnout and start feeling more in control and hopeful about their future.

## 1. The Victim Mindset

The victim mindset is a common trap that individuals fall into when they're feeling burned out. It's characterized by thoughts and beliefs that suggest that one's circumstances are outside of their control and that they're powerless to change them. This mindset can lead to feelings of hopelessness, helplessness, and resignation. It's important to recognize that this mindset is not only unproductive but also harmful. It prevents individuals from taking action to improve their situation and instead, perpetuates the cycle of burnout.

## 2. The Empowered Mindset

In contrast to the victim mindset, the empowered mindset is characterized by a belief in one's ability to make choices and take actions that can improve their present and future. It's the belief that one has the power to change their circumstances and that they're not bound by their current situation. This mindset is not about denying the challenges that exist, but rather about recognizing that there are always options and possibilities for change.

## 3. Taking Action

One of the key differences between the victim and empowered mindset is the willingness to take action. When individuals are feeling burned out, it's easy to feel overwhelmed and unsure of where to start. However, taking small actions can help individuals begin to feel more in control and hopeful about their situation. Some examples of actions that can be taken include:

- *Increasing attentiveness to physical and emotional needs*: This can include getting more sleep, taking breaks during the workday, and engaging in self-care activities such as exercise or meditation.

- *Re-evaluating commitments*: Consider whether there are commitments that can be reduced or eliminated, such as taking a break from a volunteer position or delegating tasks to others.

- *Seeking support*: Reach out to friends, family, or a therapist for emotional support and to talk through challenges and stressors.

- *Setting boundaries*: Learn to say no to requests that are not aligned with priorities or that add to an already heavy workload.

## 4. Challenging Assumptions

Often, the victim mindset is fueled by assumptions about what's possible and what's not. It's important to challenge these assumptions and consider whether they're based in reality or if they're self-imposed limitations. For example, an individual may assume that they cannot take a vacation because they have too much work to do, but upon further examination, they may realize that they can take a few days off and delegate tasks to others.

## 5. The Role of Mindset in Burnout Recovery

The mindset that an individual has when approaching burnout recovery can greatly impact their success. An empowered mindset allows individuals to see that they have options and that they can take actions to improve their situation. It also helps individuals to be more resilient and adaptable, which are key components of burnout recovery.

## Conclusion

Burnout can be a debilitating experience, but it's important to remember that individuals have the power to take control of their situation and start feeling less burned out. By shifting from a victim mindset to an empowered one, individuals can begin to take action and make changes that improve their physical, emotional, and mental well-being. It's not always easy, but it's worth it. Remember, small actions can lead to big changes, and a shift in mindset can be the first step towards a healthier, happier life.

ACHIEVING YOUR FULL POTENTIAL

# Chapter 5

## From Languishing to Flourishing: 3 Steps to Find Meaning in Your Career

Are you feeling unfulfilled and disconnected from your work? Do you struggle to find meaning and purpose in your daily tasks? If so, you're not alone. Many people, especially those just starting out in their careers, experience a sense of languishing – a feeling of being stuck and unfulfilled. However, it's important to remember that you don't have to stay in this rut. With the right strategies and mindset, you can break free from languishing and start flourishing in your career.

In this chapter, we will explore three steps to help you do just that.

**Step 1: Set Boundaries**

The first step to stopping languishing is to set boundaries. This means establishing clear limits on your time, energy, and emotions, and making space for reflection and planning. When you set boundaries, you're able to protect your most valuable resources and focus on what's truly important to you.

One way to set boundaries is to identify areas where you're feeling resentful or frustrated. Ask yourself, "Where am I feeling resentment and frustration regarding my time and energy?" Once you've identified these areas, you can start setting boundaries to protect yourself. For example, you might set a boundary around your work hours, refusing to work late nights or weekends unless absolutely necessary. Or, you might set a boundary around your energy, saying no to tasks that drain you and focusing on tasks that energize you.

Setting boundaries also allows you to make time for reflection and planning. By setting aside dedicated time for reflection, you can step back from the daily grind and think about your long-term goals and aspirations. This can help you identify areas where you want to grow and change, and make a plan to get there.

## Step 2: Reflect on Your Path, Success, and Mission

Once you've set boundaries and made time for reflection, the next step is to reflect on your current path, success, and mission. This means taking a step back and assessing how you got to where you are today, what success looks like for you, and what values are most important to you right now.

Start by asking yourself some questions:

- How did I get here? What choices and experiences led me to this point in my career?

- What does success look like for me? What are my goals and aspirations?

- What are the values that are most important to me right now? What kind of work environment and culture align with these values?

Reflecting on these questions can help you identify any disconnect between your current reality and your ideal career path. You might find that you're on the right path, but there are certain aspects of your job that aren't aligned with your values or goals. Or, you might realize that you're on the wrong path altogether and need to make a change.

**Step 3: Craft Your Job**

If you've reflected on your path, success, and mission and found a disconnect between your current reality and your ideal career path, the next step is to craft your job. This means proactively taking steps to improve your happiness at work and align your job with your values and goals.

One way to craft your job is to identify aspects of your work that align with your values and goals, and focus on these areas. For example, if you're a writer and your company's mission aligns with your personal values, you might focus on writing articles that support this mission. Or, if you're a software developer and you're passionate about innovation, you might seek out projects that allow you to work on cutting-edge technology.

Another way to craft your job is to seek out new opportunities within your current company. You might talk to your manager about taking on new responsibilities or switching to a different role that aligns more closely with your interests and strengths. Or, you might seek out opportunities to work on cross-functional teams or projects that allow you to learn new skills and expand your network.

**Conclusion**

Feeling unfulfilled and disconnected from your work can be a challenging and demotivating experience. However, by setting boundaries, reflecting on your path, success, and mission, and crafting your job, you can break free from languishing and start flourishing in your career. Remember, it's never too early or too late to take control of your career and make a change. By taking proactive steps to improve your happiness and alignment at work, you can find meaning, purpose, and fulfillment in your career.

# ACHIEVING YOUR FULL POTENTIAL

# ACHIEVING YOUR FULL POTENTIAL

# ACHIEVING YOUR FULL POTENTIAL

# Part 2

## Early Career Development

# ACHIEVING YOUR FULL POTENTIAL

# Chapter 6

## Growing Your Career in a Virtual World: Tips for Young Workers

In the past, building a successful career often relied heavily on in-person networking experiences. However, with the rise of remote work, young workers may find it challenging to develop their professional networks and grow in their careers. The good news is that there are still plenty of opportunities to build relationships, learn new skills, and advance in your career, even in a virtual environment.

In this chapter, we will explore some effective ways to grow in your career as a young worker in a virtual world.

## Strategies to Take Advantage of Virtual Opportunities

Let's face it, the world of work is changing fast, and it can be tough to know how to grow and succeed in a virtual environment. In this section, we'll explore four effective ways to grow in your career as a young worker in a virtual world.

*1. Treat Virtual Team Meetings as Networking Opportunities*

Virtual team meetings can be a great way to connect with your colleagues and build relationships. Make an effort to join the meeting a few minutes early and strike up a conversation with other team members. You can talk about anything from your weekend plans to your current projects, and even share your interests and hobbies. By doing so, you'll establish a personal connection with your colleagues and create a sense of camaraderie, which can help you build a strong foundation for your virtual network.

*2. Find a Mentor*

Having a mentor can be incredibly valuable for young workers, as they can provide guidance, support, and valuable insights into your industry. While it may seem challenging to find a mentor in a virtual environment, there are several ways to do so. You can start by looking into your alumni network or signing up for workshops in your areas of interest. Attend virtual events and join online communities related to your field, where you can connect with experienced professionals who can offer advice and mentorship.

*3. Take Initiative*

Taking initiative is a great way to build your skills, demonstrate your value to your team, and make a positive impact on your organization. Look for ways to help your team members using your talents and strengths. For example, if you're great at presentations, offer to help a peer step up their game in their next PowerPoint. By taking the initiative, you'll not only build relationships with your colleagues but also show your willingness to go above and beyond, which can help you stand out in a virtual environment.

*4. Say Yes to Stretch Assignments*

Stretch assignments are an excellent way to build new skills and meet people from other departments. When you're given the opportunity to work on a project outside of your comfort zone, embrace it. Not only will you learn new skills, but you'll also demonstrate your willingness to take on new challenges and show your commitment to your career growth.

## Specific Ways Young Workers Can Demonstrate Initiative in a Virtual Work Setting

As a virtual worker, it's important to show initiative and take the lead on projects and tasks. Here are some other ways young workers can demonstrate initiative in a virtual work setting:

1. *Be proactive*: Anticipate what needs to be done and take the initiative to do it. For example, if you notice a task is falling behind schedule, offer to help out or take the lead on it.

2. *Offer to help others*: If you see a colleague struggling with a task, offer to lend a hand. This not only shows initiative but also helps build a strong team dynamic.

3. *Take ownership of your work*: Don't wait for someone to tell you what to do. Take ownership of your projects and tasks, and take the initiative to ensure they're completed to the best of your ability.

4. *Look for opportunities to innovate*: Virtual work environments can be a great opportunity to try new

things and innovate. Look for ways to streamline processes, improve communication, or automate tasks.

5. *Communicate effectively*: Communication is key in a virtual work environment. Make sure to communicate clearly and effectively with your team, and take the initiative to ask questions or clarify tasks when needed.

6. *Be flexible*: Virtual work can be unpredictable, and things don't always go as planned. Be flexible and adaptable, and take the initiative to adjust your schedule or work style as needed.

7. *Show enthusiasm and energy*: Even though you're not in the same physical space as your colleagues, it's important to show your enthusiasm and energy. This can help to boost team morale and motivation.

8. *Take the initiative to learn*: Virtual work environments can be a great opportunity to learn new skills and expand your knowledge. Take the initiative to watch webinars, attend virtual training sessions, or read industry blogs to stay up-to-date.

By following these tips, young workers can demonstrate initiative in a virtual work setting and show their colleagues and superiors that they're committed to their work and their career.

## Conclusion

Growing your career in a virtual world may require some adjustments, but it's still possible to build a strong professional network and advance in your career. By treating virtual team meetings as networking opportunities, finding a mentor, taking initiative, and saying yes to stretch assignments, you'll be well on your way to success. Remember, the key is to be proactive, engaged, and open to new opportunities. With the right mindset and approach, you can thrive in a virtual environment and build a fulfilling career.

# ACHIEVING YOUR FULL POTENTIAL

# ACHIEVING YOUR FULL POTENTIAL

# Chapter 7

## Taking Control of Your Onboarding: A Guide to Success in Your New Job

Starting a new job can be both exciting and intimidating. You want to make a good impression, learn as much as possible, and hit the ground running. However, relying solely on your company's onboarding process may not be enough to ensure your success. To truly excel in your new role, it's important to take control of your integration and proactively cultivate connections, ask the right questions, and build trust.

In this chapter, we will explore how to take control of our onboarding process and provide detailed examples to help you get off to a strong start.

**Cultivating Connections**

One of the most important things you can do when starting a new job is to cultivate connections up, down, and across. This means building relationships with your supervisor, colleagues, and other stakeholders who can help you succeed in your role. To do this, start by identifying the influencers in your department and organization. These are the people who have a significant impact on the work that you do and can provide valuable insight and guidance.

For example, if you're starting a new job as a marketing manager, you might identify the head of sales, the product development team, and the customer service department as key influencers. Spend time getting to know them face-to-face, ask questions about their goals and challenges, and look for ways to collaborate and support each other. By building these relationships early on, you'll be better positioned to navigate the organization and get the support you need to succeed.

## Asking Questions

Another important aspect of taking control of your onboarding is asking the right questions. Your boss can be a valuable resource in helping you understand how you'll be evaluated and identifying early wins. Don't be afraid to ask questions like:

- What are the key performance indicators (KPIs) for my role?

- What are the biggest challenges facing the team right now?

- What are some early wins that I can achieve to demonstrate my value to the organization?

By asking these questions, you'll have a better understanding of what's expected of you and how you can make a positive impact. Additionally, your boss will appreciate your proactive approach and willingness to learn.

## Looking for Projects

In addition to building relationships and asking questions, look for projects that will motivate the team, can be achieved quickly, and deliver operational or financial results.

These projects can help you build credibility and demonstrate your value to the organization.

For example, if you're starting a new job as a project manager, you might look for projects that can be completed within the first 90 days. These projects could include streamlining a process, implementing a new tool, or completing a small-scale pilot project. By focusing on these types of projects, you'll be able to achieve quick wins and build momentum for larger initiatives down the line.

**Building Trust**

Finally, it's important to build trust with your colleagues and supervisor. This can be done by being honest about the challenges you see and being transparent in your communication. Don't try to sugarcoat issues or pretend like everything is fine when it's not. Instead, address challenges head-on and work collaboratively with your team to find solutions.

For example, if you notice that there's a lack of clear communication between departments, bring it up in a respectful and constructive way. Propose solutions like regular meetings or a shared project management tool to help improve communication and collaboration. By building trust and demonstrating your commitment to the team's success, you'll be able to work more effectively and achieve better results.

## Conclusion

Starting a new job can be a daunting experience, but by taking control of your onboarding, you can set yourself up for success. By cultivating connections up, down, and across, asking the right questions, looking for projects that deliver results, and building trust, you'll be able to hit the ground running and make a positive impact on your organization. Remember, it's up to you to take control of your integration and proactively drive your success.

# ACHIEVING YOUR FULL POTENTIAL

# Chapter 8

## Navigating the Workplace: Strategies for Advancing Your Career

In today's fast-paced and competitive job market, it's no secret that hard work alone isn't enough to get ahead. In her article, "How to Showcase Your Potential as a Leader," Tutti Taygerly highlights three key strategies that can help individuals advance their careers and reach their full potential. These strategies include moving from performance currency to relationship currency, setting boundaries around low-value work, and advocating for more of the work you want.

In this chapter, we will take a closer look at each of these strategies and provide examples of how they can be applied in real-life scenarios.

## Move from Performance Currency to Relationship Currency

In technical fields, workers are often initially assessed based on their performance currency, or how well they deliver on assigned tasks. However, to advance in your career, it's important to move beyond just delivering results and start investing in the people around you. This is where relationship currency comes in. Relationship currency involves building strong connections with your colleagues, leaders, and other professionals in your industry.

One way to start building relationship currency is to ask a colleague to join you for a virtual coffee or invite a leader you admire out to lunch. These informal meetings can help you build a connection with your colleagues and leaders, and allow you to learn more about their interests, goals, and challenges. By showing genuine interest in others, you can establish a foundation for a strong professional relationship.

Another way to build relationship currency is to offer to help others with their work. For example, if a colleague is struggling with a project, offer to lend a hand or provide guidance. By doing so, you not only build a stronger connection with your colleague, but you also demonstrate your expertise and willingness to help others.

**Set Boundaries Around Low-Value Work**

Women, newbies, and people of color often find themselves assigned office housekeeping tasks, such as taking meeting notes or organizing social activities. While these tasks may seem harmless, they can actually drain your energy and prevent you from focusing on high-value work that will help you advance in your career.

To avoid getting trapped in this vicious cycle, it's important to set boundaries around low-value work. This means politely declining requests that don't align with your strengths or long-term goals. Instead, focus on high-value work that will help you build your skills and expertise.

For example, if your boss asks you to take meeting notes, you could respond by saying, "I understand the importance of having detailed notes, but I'm currently working on a high-priority project that requires my full attention. Would it be possible for someone else to take the notes this time?" By setting boundaries in a respectful and professional manner, you can avoid getting bogged down in low-value work and focus on high-value tasks that will help you advance in your career.

**Advocate for More of the Work You Want**

Learning how to respectfully promote your work and the value you're contributing is essential to your growth. To do this, build strong relationships with your boss and advocate for others. By doing so, you can increase your visibility and showcase your expertise to the right people.

One way to advocate for more of the work you want is to proactively seek out opportunities to work on high-profile projects. For example, you could approach your boss and say, "I've been following the progress of the new marketing campaign, and I believe I could contribute my skills and expertise to help make it a success. Would it be possible for me to join the project team?" By taking the initiative and promoting your skills, you can increase your chances of getting assigned to high-value projects that will help you advance in your career.

Another way to advocate for yourself is to highlight your achievements and the value you're bringing to the organization. For example, you could send a weekly email to your boss summarizing your accomplishments and how they're impacting the business. By doing so, you'll keep your boss informed of your progress and reinforce your value to the organization.

**Conclusion**

Advancing your career requires more than just hard work and delivering results. By moving from performance currency to relationship currency, setting boundaries around low-value work, and advocating for more of the work you want, you can increase your visibility, build strong relationships, and showcase your expertise to the right people. It's not enough to simply do good work, you need to be able to connect with others, build trust, and demonstrate your value to the organization. By doing so, you'll be well on your way to achieving your career goals and making a meaningful impact in your field. Remember, it's not just about working hard, it's about working smart and building meaningful connections that will help you succeed.

# ACHIEVING YOUR FULL POTENTIAL

# Chapter 9

## Unlocking the Power of Personal Motivation: Strategies for Success When You Just Don't Want To

As professionals, we've all been there - the feeling of dread that comes with facing a daunting task or the lack of motivation to tackle a project that seems insurmountable. It's easy to get caught up in the daily grind and lose sight of our goals, or worse, feel like we're just going through the motions. But what if we could break free from this cycle and reignite our passion for our work? The answer lies in unlocking our personal motivation.

In this chapter, we will explore strategies for overcoming a lack of motivation and cultivating a mindset that drive success.

**Identify Your Why**

Before we dive into strategies, it's essential to understand the foundation of personal motivation - our "why." Our "why" is the reason we get out of bed in the morning, the purpose that drives us, and the passion that fuels our work. According to Simon Sinek, author of Start with Why, "People don't buy what you do; they buy why you do it." (Sinek, 2011) Understanding our "why" gives us a sense of direction, helps us stay focused, and provides the motivation to push through challenges.

To discover your "why," ask yourself:

- What are my core values and beliefs?

- What problem am I trying to solve in my work?

- What impact do I want to make?

- What gets me excited about my work?

**Set Meaningful Goals**

Once you have a clear understanding of your "why," it's time to set meaningful goals. Goal setting is a powerful tool for motivation, but it's essential to set goals that align with your "why." Meaningful goals are specific, measurable, achievable, relevant, and time-bound (SMART). They should also be challenging enough to inspire growth but not so daunting that they become discouraging.

For example, instead of setting a goal to "be more productive," set a goal to "increase productivity by 20% within the next 6 months by implementing a time management system and prioritizing tasks based on importance and urgency."

**Create a Positive Work Environment**

Our work environment plays a significant role in our motivation. A positive work environment can inspire creativity, foster collaboration, and enhance productivity. Here are some ways to create a positive work environment:

- *Declutter your workspace*: A cluttered workspace can contribute to feeling overwhelmed and unproductive. Take the time to organize your workspace, and make it visually appealing.

- *Add plants*: Plants not only purify the air, but they also create a calming atmosphere.

- *Incorporate ergonomic furniture*: Invest in ergonomic furniture that promotes comfort and reduces eye strain.

- *Play music*: Music can boost mood and productivity. Create a playlist that motivates you and helps you focus.

## Eliminate Distractions

Distractions are productivity killers. They can derail our focus and hinder our progress. Here are some ways to eliminate distractions:

- *Turn off notifications*: Turn off notifications on your phone, computer, or any other device that can distract you from your work.

- *Use a website blocker*: Tools like Freedom or SelfControl can block distracting websites for a set period, helping you stay focused.

- *Schedule breaks*: Schedule breaks throughout the day to recharge and refocus.

**Practice Self-Care**

Self-care is essential for maintaining motivation. It's challenging to be productive and motivated when we're exhausted, stressed, or burned out. Here are some self-care strategies:

- *Exercise*: Regular exercise can boost energy levels, reduce stress, and enhance cognitive function.

- *Meditation*: Meditation can help calm the mind, increase focus, and promote relaxation.

- *Sleep*: Adequate sleep is crucial for productivity and motivation. Aim for 7-8 hours of sleep each night.

**Seek Accountability**

Another way to seek accountability is to join a community of like-minded individuals who share your goals and values. This could be a mastermind group, a networking group, or even an online community. Share your goals and progress with the group, and ask them to hold you accountable. This can provide an added motivation to stay on track, as you won't want to disappoint your peers.

Finally, consider hiring a coach or mentor who can provide guidance and accountability. A coach can help you set and achieve your goals, and provide support and encouragement along the way.

## Conclusion

Staying motivated and achieving our goals requires a combination of the right mindset, habits, and support systems. By implementing the strategies outlined in this article, you'll be well on your way to staying motivated and achieving your goals. Remember to celebrate your successes along the way, and don't be too hard on yourself when you encounter setbacks. With persistence, determination, and the right support, you can achieve anything you set your mind to.

# ACHIEVING YOUR FULL POTENTIAL

ns-serif"># ACHIEVING YOUR FULL POTENTIAL

# Chapter 10

## Overcoming Imposter Syndrome: Building Confidence in Your Career

Imposter syndrome can be a crippling experience, causing doubt and insecurity to cloud our minds and hinder our professional growth. However, by acknowledging its normalcy and implementing strategies to combat it, we can overcome this self-critical mindset and thrive in our careers.

In this chapter, we will explore practical ways to dial down self-doubt, build confidence, and find support in our professional journeys.

**Acknowledge and Embrace Newness**

Feeling nervous and uncertain in a new role or when surrounded by individuals who differ from us is natural. By recognizing this, we can better navigate the challenges and build resilience. Remember, being new or a minority among a group does not define our worth or capabilities. Instead, it presents an opportunity for growth and learning.

**Conquer the Fear of Failure**

Imposter syndrome often stems from a deep-rooted fear of failure. To overcome this fear, we must shift our perspective and view failure as a steppingstone towards success. Instead of letting fear paralyze us, channel your nervous energy into learning and adding value to your new role. Embrace challenges as opportunities for growth and improvement.

**Embrace Authenticity**

Being sincere to ourselves and others is vital in combating imposter syndrome. When we are clear about our values, strengths, and personal identity, we are less likely to conform to societal expectations or try to fit into a mold that wasn't designed for us. Embrace your uniqueness and let it shine in your work. Authenticity breeds confidence and attracts opportunities that align with our true selves.

**Capitalize on Your Strengths**

No one has all the answers, and that's perfectly okay. Recognize that you were selected for your role based on your unique strengths and abilities. Focus on utilizing these strengths to make a meaningful impact. By capitalizing on what sets us apart, we can contribute value and gain confidence in our abilities.

**Find an Ally**

Even with the implementation of the above strategies, imposter syndrome may still persist. In such cases, it can be immensely helpful to seek out an ally or a support system. Allies can provide a safe space for sharing experiences and offering encouragement. Look for individuals who understand your journey, have faced similar challenges, and can provide guidance and reassurance.

## Conclusion

Imposter syndrome can be debilitating, hindering our professional growth and happiness. However, by acknowledging its existence and implementing strategies to combat it, we can overcome self-doubt and thrive in our careers. Embrace the newness, conquer the fear of failure, be authentic, capitalize on your strengths, and find support in the form of allies. Remember, you are deserving of success, and by embracing your true self, you can achieve your career aspirations with confidence and fulfillment.

# ACHIEVING YOUR FULL POTENTIAL

## ACHIEVING YOUR FULL POTENTIAL

# Part 3

# Career Navigation and Improvement

# ACHIEVING YOUR FULL POTENTIAL

# Chapter 11

## Breaking Free from a Toxic Work Environment: Strategies for Leaving a Bad Job

Are you feeling trapped in a job that's sucking the life out of you? Do you find yourself constantly stressed, anxious, or depressed due to a toxic work environment? If so, you're not alone. Many people struggle to leave a bad job, and it's not always easy to understand why.

In this chapter, we will explore five common reasons it's hard to leave a bad job and provide strategies for moving on.

## Reason 1: Fear of the Unknown

One of the biggest reasons people stay in a bad job is the fear of the unknown. The thought of leaving a secure job, even a toxic one, can be daunting. You may worry about finding a new job, paying bills, or maintaining your lifestyle. The fear of the unknown can paralyze you, making it difficult to take the first step towards change.

Addressing this fear head-on is crucial. Start by creating a plan for your next career move. Update your resume, LinkedIn profile, and networking skills. Research job opportunities and industries that align with your values and interests. Consider taking courses or attending workshops to enhance your skills and increase your confidence. By taking small steps towards a new career, you'll feel more in control and prepared for the unknown.

## Reason 2: Financial Constraints

Financial constraints are another significant reason people stay in a bad job. You may feel trapped due to financial responsibilities, such as a mortgage, car payment, or family to support. The thought of taking a pay cut or risking a new job with a lower salary can be unbearable.

It's essential to prioritize your well-being and long-term financial stability. Consider taking a temporary pay cut or salary reduction to escape a toxic work environment. Create a budget and savings plan to ensure you have enough money to cover expenses during the transition. Look for new job opportunities that offer growth potential, as a lower starting salary may lead to higher earnings in the long run.

**Reason 3: Lack of Self-Confidence**

A toxic work environment can erode your self-confidence, making it challenging to leave. You may feel like you're not good enough or that you'll never find a better job. The fear of failure can hold you back from pursuing new opportunities.

Rebuilding your self-confidence is vital. Focus on your strengths and accomplishments. List your achievements and positive experiences, no matter how small. Practice positive self-talk, and seek support from friends, family, or a therapist. Take on new challenges, such as volunteering or taking a course, to enhance your skills and boost your confidence.

## Reason 4: Sense of Obligation

You may feel a sense of obligation to your employer, colleagues, or clients, making it difficult to leave. Perhaps you've invested years of your life in the company, or you feel responsible for your team's success.

It's essential to remember that your well-being is crucial. Acknowledge your feelings of obligation but prioritize your health and happiness. Set boundaries and communicate your needs to your employer or colleagues. If possible, negotiate a flexible work arrangement or discuss a transition plan that works for everyone.

## Reason 5: Lack of Awareness

Sometimes, people stay in a bad job due to a lack of awareness. You may not realize the impact of the toxic work environment on your mental and physical health or that there are better job opportunities available.

Educate yourself on the signs of a toxic work environment and the benefits of leaving. Research job opportunities and salaries in your industry. Seek advice from mentors, career coaches, or friends who have successfully transitioned to new jobs.

## Conclusion

Leaving a bad job is never easy, but it's essential for your well-being and career growth. By understanding the reasons that keep you stuck and implementing strategies to overcome them, you'll be empowered to take control of your career. Remember, it's okay to take time to reflect, regroup, and explore new opportunities. You deserve a job that aligns with your values, supports your growth, and fosters a healthy work environment. Take the first step today and start your journey towards a fulfilling career.

ACHIEVING YOUR FULL POTENTIAL

# Chapter 12

# The Myth of 100% Motivation: Why You're Probably Under-Performing at Work and How to Fix It

Are you tired of feeling like you're not living up to your full potential at work? Do you sometimes feel like you're just going through the motions, unable to tap into your true talents and abilities? If so, you're not alone. Research suggests that few individuals are 100% motivated throughout sustained periods at work. In fact, even if you think you're performing to the best of your capabilities, chances are you're wrong. There's a gap between what people think of their performance and how they actually perform, and it's wider than you might think.

The reasons for this gap are varied and complex, but they can be boiled down to four main factors: (1) poor fit, (2) disengagement, (3) organizational politics, and (4) personal circumstances.

In this chapter, we'll explore each of these factors in-depth and provide practical tips for overcoming them. By understanding the invisible forces that govern the dynamics of organizations and optimizing your job to fit with your interests, beliefs, and broader life activities, you can unlock your full potential and perform to the best of your abilities.

## 1. Poor Fit: Talent is Mainly Personality in the Right Place

Have you ever felt like a square peg in a round hole? If so, you know what it's like to be in a job that's not a good fit. When your personality, values, and work style don't align with your job and organization, it's like trying to force a puzzle piece into the wrong spot. No matter how hard you try, it just won't fit.

# ACHIEVING YOUR FULL POTENTIAL

A poor fit between an individual's strengths, weaknesses, and interests and the requirements and culture of the job can lead to disengagement and underperformance. When an individual's skills and abilities are not aligned with the demands of the job, they may feel unchallenged, unfulfilled, or even overwhelmed. This can result in a lack of motivation, decreased productivity, and a higher likelihood of turnover.

For example, an individual who is highly creative and enjoys generating new ideas may struggle in a role that requires repetitive, routine tasks. Similarly, an individual who is detail-oriented and enjoys analyzing data may not thrive in a role that requires a lot of public speaking and networking.

A poor fit can also lead to a lack of engagement and satisfaction with one's job, which can affect an individual's mental and physical well-being. Research has shown that employees who are unhappy in their jobs are more likely to experience stress, burnout, and other negative emotions, which can impact their overall health and well-being.

Furthermore, a poor fit can also impact an individual's career advancement and opportunities for growth. If an individual is not performing well in their current role, they may not be considered for promotions or other opportunities within the organization. This can limit their career advancement and earning potential, which can have long-term consequences for their professional and personal life.

To avoid a poor fit, it is essential for individuals to carefully consider their strengths, weaknesses, and interests when choosing a career path or job opportunity. They should also research the job requirements, culture, and values of the organization to ensure that they align with their own goals and values. Employers can also play a role by providing clear job descriptions, offering opportunities for professional development, and fostering a positive work culture that supports employee engagement and satisfaction.

Poor fit between an individual's strengths, weaknesses, and interests and the requirements and culture of the job can have significant consequences for both the individual and the organization. It is essential for individuals to carefully consider their strengths, weaknesses, and interests when choosing a career path or job opportunity, and for employers to provide a supportive work environment that fosters employee engagement and satisfaction.

## 2. Disengagement: Finding Time to Be Curious and Learn, Connecting with Colleagues, and Talking to Your Boss

Disengagement refers to a state of being disconnected or disenchanted with one's job or work environment. It's a common problem in many organizations, and it can have negative consequences for both employees and employers.

There are several reasons why employees may become disengaged at work. Some of the most common causes include:

1. *Lack of challenge or meaningful work*: Employees who feel like they're not being challenged or that their work isn't meaningful may become disengaged.

2. *Poor management or leadership*: Employees who feel like their manager or leadership team is ineffective, unsupportive, or uncommunicative may become disengaged.

3. *Lack of recognition or rewards*: Employees who feel like their efforts are not recognized or rewarded may become disengaged.

4. *Poor work-life balance*: Employees who feel like they're overworked, undervalued, or that their work is

impacting their personal life in a negative way may become disengaged.

5. *Lack of opportunities for growth and development*: Employees who feel like they're not learning or growing in their role may become disengaged.

Disengagement can manifest in a variety of ways, including:

1. *Decreased productivity*: Disengaged employees may produce less work or produce work of lower quality.

2. *Absenteeism or tardiness*: Disengaged employees may miss or be late to work more frequently.

3. *Lack of motivation*: Disengaged employees may lack the motivation to take on new projects or tasks.

4. *Negative attitude*: Disengaged employees may express negative views about the organization or their colleagues.

5. *Turnover*: Disengaged employees may ultimately leave the organization.

To address disengagement, organizations can take several steps, such as:

1. Regularly surveying employees to understand their concerns and needs.

2. Providing opportunities for growth and development.

3. Recognizing and rewarding employee achievements.

4. Encouraging open communication and feedback.

5. Fostering a positive work culture that values and supports employees.

Disengagement is a common problem in many organizations that can have negative consequences for both employees and employers. By understanding the causes of disengagement and taking steps to address it, organizations can create a more positive and productive work environment.

## 3. Organizational Politics: It's Naïve to Think That You Can Let Your Talents Speak for Themselves

Organizational politics refers to the informal power dynamics and social structures that exist within an organization. It is a natural aspect of any group of people working together, and it can have a significant impact on an individual's performance and success within the organization.

In any organization, there are individuals who have more power and influence than others. This power and influence can be based on a variety of factors such as job title, seniority, personal relationships, and expertise. These individuals may use their power and influence to shape the organization's culture, make decisions, and advance their own careers.

Organizational politics can manifest in various ways, such as:

1. *Gossip and rumors*: Gossip and rumors can spread quickly through an organization, and they can have a significant impact on an individual's reputation and relationships.

2. *Cliques and factions*: Cliques and factions can form within an organization, with individuals forming alliances and coalitions to advance their own interests.

3. *Power struggles*: Power struggles can occur when individuals or groups compete for limited resources, recognition, or influence within the organization.

4. *Favoritism and nepotism*: Favoritism and nepotism can occur when individuals in positions of power use their influence to promote or advance their friends, family members, or other favored individuals.

5. *Information hoarding:* Information hoarding can occur when individuals or groups withhold information or resources from others in order to maintain their power and influence.

To successfully navigate organizational politics, individuals can take several steps:

1. *Observe and listen:* It's important to observe and listen to the dynamics within the organization to understand the power structures and relationships at play.

2. *Build relationships:* Building relationships with key individuals within the organization can help to increase one's influence and access to information.

3. *Communicate effectively:* Effective communication is key to building relationships and advancing one's interests within the organization.

4. *Be strategic:* It's important to be strategic in one's actions and decisions, taking into account the potential impact on one's career and relationships within the organization.

5. *Seek mentorship*: Seeking mentorship from individuals who have successfully navigated the organization's politics can provide valuable insights and guidance.

6. *Be adaptable*: It's important to be adaptable and flexible in response to changing power dynamics and political structures within the organization.

7. *Maintain integrity*: It's important to maintain one's integrity and values in the face of organizational politics, avoiding behaviors that could compromise one's professionalism or reputation.

Organizational politics is a natural aspect of any organization, and it can have a significant impact on an individual's performance and success. By understanding the power dynamics at play and taking steps to navigate them effectively, individuals can increase their influence and achieve their career goals.

## 4. Personal Circumstances: No Matter How Engaged and Talented Someone Is, Personal Drawbacks and Setbacks Will Often Interfere with Their Career Success

Personal circumstances can have a significant impact on an individual's performance at work. These circumstances can include a range of factors such as health issues, family responsibilities, financial stress, and other personal problems.

When an individual is facing personal challenges, it can be difficult to focus and be productive at work.

Health issues, for example, can affect an individual's ability to perform physically or mentally. Chronic illnesses, disabilities, or temporary health problems can make it challenging to meet job demands, leading to decreased productivity and performance. Mental health issues such as depression, anxiety, or stress can also impact an individual's ability to concentrate and focus, leading to decreased work performance.

Family responsibilities can also impact an individual's work performance. For example, an individual who is a primary caregiver for a family member may need to take time off work to care for their loved one, leading to decreased productivity. Additionally, family problems such as divorce, childcare issues, or elder care can cause stress and distraction, making it challenging to focus on work responsibilities.

Financial stress is another personal circumstance that can impact work performance. Financial problems can cause an individual to feel anxious or worried, leading to decreased focus and productivity. Additionally, financial stress can lead to absenteeism or tardiness due to issues such as car trouble or transportation costs.

Other personal problems such as relationship issues, substance abuse, or legal problems can also affect an individual's work performance. These issues can cause stress, anxiety, or depression, leading to decreased productivity and performance.

To overcome personal circumstances that are impacting work performance, individuals can take several steps. These steps include:

1. *Seek support:* Individuals should seek support from family, friends, or professional counselors to help them manage their personal problems.

2. Communicate with the employer: Individuals should communicate with their employer about their personal circumstances and seek accommodations such as flexible work arrangements or time off when needed.

3. *Prioritize self-care*: Individuals should prioritize self-care by taking care of their physical and mental health, exercising regularly, and engaging in stress-reducing activities.

4. *Seek help from employee assistance programs*: Many employers offer employee assistance programs that provide resources and support for employees facing personal challenges.

5. *Consider a job change*: If personal circumstances are impacting work performance, and the individual cannot resolve the issues, it may be time to consider a job change.

Personal circumstances can significantly impact an individual's performance at work. It is essential for individuals to recognize the impact of personal problems on their work and seek support and resources to manage these challenges. Employers can also play a critical role in supporting employees by providing resources and accommodations to help them manage personal circumstances that may be impacting their work performance.

## Conclusion

It is important to recognize that talent alone is not enough to excel and impress in the workplace. Optimizing job fit, maintaining curiosity, navigating organizational politics, and managing personal circumstances are all critical factors in unleashing one's true potential. By aligning interests, beliefs, and broader life activities with work, individuals can create a harmonious environment that promotes their growth and allows them to perform to the best of their capabilities. Remember, self-reflection and self-awareness are key to understanding your own performance and identifying areas for improvement. By continuously evaluating and adapting, individuals can overcome obstacles and unlock their true potential in the workplace.

# Chapter 13

## Making Better Career Decisions: A 5-Step Framework

Making decisions can be a daunting task, especially when it comes to career choices. With so many factors to consider and various stakeholders involved, it's easy to feel overwhelmed and uncertain. However, by following a structured framework, you can simplify the process and make informed decisions that align with your values and goals.

In this chapter, we will explore a 5-step framework to help you make better career decisions.

## Step 1: What are your feelings telling you?

The first step in making better career decisions is to understand your feelings about your current job or the career path you're considering. Take some time to reflect on your emotions and jot down different careers that come to mind. Ask yourself questions like:

- What are the things I enjoy doing the most in my current job?

- Are there any tasks or responsibilities that I find unfulfilling or uninteresting?

- What are my long-term career goals, and do they align with my current job?

By examining your feelings, you'll get a better understanding of what you want and don't want in a career. This information will help you narrow down your options and focus on careers that align with your interests and aspirations.

## Step 2: What matters to you?

Understanding your values is crucial in making career decisions that align with your personal and professional goals. Take a psychological assessment or complete an exercise that helps you identify your values. Consider questions like:

- What motivates me?

- What do I value most in my work?

- What kind of work environment do I thrive in?

Once you have a clear understanding of your values, you can use them as a benchmark to evaluate potential career paths. This will help you make choices that are fulfilling and meaningful, rather than just focusing on salary or job title.

## Step 3: What matters to other people?

While it's important to prioritize your own values and goals, it's also essential to consider how your career decisions will impact your loved ones. Ask for their thoughts, input, and feelings about your career choices. This will help you:

- Gain different perspectives and insights

- Understand how your decisions will affect your personal relationships

- Make decisions that are beneficial to both you and your loved ones

**Step 4: What is the reality of the situation?**

It's easy to get caught up in assumptions and misconceptions about certain career paths. However, it's important to be objective and consider the realities of each option. Research the job market, salary ranges, and required skills for each career you're considering. Ask yourself questions like:

- What are the job prospects and growth opportunities in this field?

- Is the salary range aligned with my financial goals and expectations?

- Do I have the necessary skills and qualifications for this career?

By understanding the realities of each career path, you can make informed decisions that are grounded in facts, rather than assumptions.

## Step 5: How do I put the pieces together?

Once you've answered the previous four questions, it's time to review all the information you've gathered. Consider how your feelings, values, loved ones' input, and the realities of each career path align. Use this information to make a final decision that aligns with your personal and professional goals.

## Conclusion

Making better career decisions requires a structured approach that considers various factors. By following the 5-step framework outlined in this article, you'll be able to:

- Identify your feelings and values

- Understand the impact on your loved ones

- Evaluate the realities of each career path

- Make informed decisions that align with your goals

Remember, career decisions are personal and can have a significant impact on your life. By taking the time to reflect, research, and evaluate your options, you'll be able to make choices that are fulfilling, meaningful, and aligned with your values.

# ACHIEVING YOUR FULL POTENTIAL

# Chapter 14

# Navigating the Workplace: Strategies for Advancing Your Career

In today's fast-paced and competitive job market, it's easy to feel like success is reserved for a select few who have it all figured out. However, the truth is that luck plays a significant role in our career paths, and sometimes, the most unexpected opportunities can lead to the most fulfilling and successful outcomes. The concept of serendipity, or the art of finding happy accidents, can help you cultivate luck and achieve your career goals.

In this chapter, we will explore the power of serendipity in your career and provide practical tips on how to cultivate it.

**Trust Serendipity: Let Go of Your Idealized Future**

One of the biggest obstacles to serendipity is our tendency to have a fixed vision of our future. We often imagine a specific job title, industry, or company that we believe is perfect for us, and we may overlook opportunities that don't fit this idealized version. To overcome this, it's essential to let go of your preconceived notions and trust that serendipity will lead you to unexpected but fulfilling opportunities.

For example, Sarah, a recent graduate, always dreamed of working in the marketing department of a big tech company. She applied to countless job openings but kept getting rejected. One day, while volunteering at a local non-profit, she met a graphic designer who introduced her to the world of design. Sarah discovered that her creative skills were a perfect fit for the design industry, and she landed a job at a small design firm that eventually led to a successful career.

## Practice Serendipitous Networking

Networking is a crucial aspect of career development, but it's essential to approach it with a mindset of serendipity. Instead of focusing solely on your career goals, practice "serendipitous networking" by connecting with others for the sake of getting to know them, their perspectives, and their stories. Attend networking events, join professional organizations, and engage in conversations with people from diverse backgrounds. You never know who might introduce you to your future employer or mentor.

Jake, a software engineer, regularly attended industry conferences and networking events. At one event, he struck up a conversation with a fellow attendee who shared his passion for artificial intelligence. They kept in touch, and a few months later, Jake received an invitation to join a startup that specialized in AI technology. He landed a senior role and helped the company secure significant funding, leading to a substantial boost in his career.

## Embrace Change and Develop New Skills

The job market is constantly evolving, and certain skills are always in demand. Embracing change and developing new skills can increase your chances of catching a lucky break.

Instead of fearing the unknown, approach change from a place of possibility and curiosity. Identify emerging trends in your industry and proactively develop skills that align with them.

Melissa, a marketing professional, noticed a growing demand for digital marketing skills. She took online courses and attended workshops to enhance her knowledge in the field. As a result, she landed a job at a prestigious marketing agency and quickly rose through the ranks.

**Trust Employers to Recognize Your Skills and Expertise**

Finally, serendipity demands that you trust something beyond yourself to tell you what's right for you. This looks like trusting employers to recognize your skills and expertise. Reach out to companies whose work and culture you find appealing, even if you don't see a specific job opening. Sometimes, a recruiter may evaluate your skills and match you to a role you were not initially interested in but that is a better fit.

Andrew, a recent college graduate, was interested in working for a non-profit organization. He reached out to several organizations and offered his volunteer services. One of the organizations recognized his passion and skill set and offered him a full-time role as a fundraising coordinator. Andrew discovered that his skills were a perfect fit for the role, and he went on to have a successful career in the non-profit sector.

**Conclusion**

Cultivating serendipity in your career requires an open mind, a willingness to take risks, and a readiness to embrace change. By letting go of your idealized future, practicing serendipitous networking, developing new skills, and trusting employers to recognize your talents, you can increase your chances of stumbling upon unexpected opportunities that may lead to success and fulfillment in your career. Remember, serendipity is not a guarantee, but by adopting these strategies, you can create an environment that fosters luck and sets you up for success. So, go ahead, take a chance, and let serendipity guide you on your career journey. You never know where it may lead you!

# ACHIEVING YOUR FULL POTENTIAL

# ACHIEVING YOUR FULL POTENTIAL

# ACHIEVING YOUR FULL POTENTIAL

# Part 4

# Expanding Your Career Impact

# ACHIEVING YOUR FULL POTENTIAL

# Chapter 15

## Building Relationships: The Key to Unlocking Career Advancement Opportunities

In today's fast-paced and competitive job market, having the right skills and experience is no longer enough to guarantee career advancement. As many individuals early in their career have discovered, it's not always the most skilled or experienced person who gets the promotion. Often, it's the person who has built strong relationships within their organization that gets noticed and selected for advancement opportunities.

In this chapter, we will explore the importance of relationships in career advancement and provide practical tips for strengthening relationships at work to increase your chances of getting promoted.

Understanding the Importance of Relationships in Career Advancement

It's a common misconception that career advancement is solely based on an individual's skills and experience. However, research has shown that relationships play a significant role in an individual's career success. A study by LinkedIn found that 85% of all jobs are filled through networking, and 70% of people were hired for a job because of a referral. These statistics highlight the importance of building strong relationships in the workplace, as they can lead to job opportunities and career advancement.

**Building Relationships with Colleagues**

The first step in building strong relationships at work is to establish good relationships with your colleagues. This can be achieved through simple acts such as saying hello in the morning, asking about their weekend, or showing an interest in their work. It's also essential to be a team player, offer to help with projects and tasks, and give credit where credit is due. By building strong relationships with your colleagues, you can create a support network that can help you navigate challenges in the workplace and advocate for you when opportunities arise.

**Building Relationships with Your Supervisor**

Building a strong relationship with your supervisor is critical to career advancement. It's essential to communicate regularly with your supervisor, keep them informed of your progress, and seek their feedback and guidance. It's also important to demonstrate your commitment to the organization and your role by taking on additional responsibilities and showing a willingness to learn and grow. By building a strong relationship with your supervisor, you can increase your visibility within the organization and demonstrate your readiness for new opportunities.

**Building Relationships with Cross-Functional Teams**

In today's collaborative work environment, it's essential to build relationships with cross-functional teams. This can be achieved through participating in company-wide initiatives, attending cross-functional meetings, and volunteering for projects that align with your interests and skills. By building relationships with cross-functional teams, you can expand your network, gain new skills and knowledge, and increase your visibility within the organization.

## Building Relationships with External Stakeholders

Finally, it's essential to build relationships with external stakeholders, such as clients, vendors, and industry leaders. This can be achieved through attending industry events, participating in professional organizations, and engaging on social media. By building relationships with external stakeholders, you can increase your knowledge of industry trends, gain new insights, and create opportunities for collaboration and career advancement.

## Conclusion

Building strong relationships is essential to career advancement. By understanding the importance of relationships in career advancement, building strong relationships with colleagues, supervisors, cross-functional teams, and external stakeholders, individuals can increase their visibility within the organization, demonstrate their readiness for new opportunities, and create a support network that can advocate for them when opportunities arise. Remember, it's not always the most skilled or experienced person who gets the promotion, it's the person who has built strong relationships within their organization that gets noticed and selected for advancement opportunities.

# ACHIEVING YOUR FULL POTENTIAL

# Chapter 16

## Millennial Managers: Driving Positive Change in the Workplace

In today's workplace, employees are no longer satisfied with just earning a paycheck. They want their work to have meaning and purpose, and they look to their leaders to provide an environment that fosters growth, autonomy, and a sense of fulfillment. Millennials, who are increasingly taking on management roles, have a unique opportunity to drive positive change within their organizations and teams.

In this chapter, we will explore five key steps that millennial managers can take to create a positive and engaging work environment that benefits both the employee and the company.

## Step 1: Be Transparent

Transparency is a cornerstone of trust and respect in any organization. When leaders are open and honest about the company's successes and challenges, it sends a message to employees that they are valued and trusted members of the team. This transparency can take many forms, such as regular town hall meetings, open-door policies, or company-wide updates on key performance indicators.

For example, at the software company, Buffer, transparency is a core value that is deeply ingrained in the company culture. The leadership team shares detailed financial reports, company goals, and even personal struggles with the entire team. This openness has created a sense of unity and shared purpose, fostering a strong team spirit and commitment to the company's mission.

## Step 2: Trust People to Work from Anywhere

In today's digital age, it's no longer necessary for employees to be tethered to their desks. With the advancement of technology, remote work has become a viable option for many companies. By trusting employees to work from anywhere, millennial managers can demonstrate their confidence in their team members' abilities and foster a sense of autonomy.

The benefits of remote work are numerous, including increased productivity, reduced commute times, and improved work-life balance. Companies like GitLab, a software development company, have embraced remote work, allowing their team members to work from anywhere in the world. This flexibility has led to increased job satisfaction, reduced turnover, and a more diverse workforce.

**Step 3: Emphasize Autonomy**

Empowering employees to take ownership of their work is a key component of a positive work environment. When leaders give their team members the freedom to make decisions and solve problems on their own, it not only increases productivity but also fosters a sense of purpose and fulfillment.

At the consulting firm, Accenture, employees are encouraged to take ownership of their projects and are given the autonomy to make decisions and suggest solutions. This approach has led to increased job satisfaction and a more engaged workforce.

## Step 4: Explain What Your Company is Doing for the Greater Good

Employees want to feel that their work is contributing to something bigger than themselves. Millennial managers can help their team members understand how their work fits into the company's larger mission and vision. This can be achieved by sharing stories of how the company's products or services are making a positive impact on society or the environment.

For example, at the outdoor apparel company, Patagonia, employees are proud to work for a company that is committed to environmental sustainability. The company's mission to reduce its carbon footprint and promote environmental responsibility resonates with its employees, who feel that their work is contributing to a greater good.

## Step 5: Focus on the Whole Employee

Finally, millennial managers should focus on the whole employee, recognizing that work-life balance is essential for job satisfaction and well-being. By offering benefits like free therapy and counseling, additional time off, or employee fitness programs, leaders can demonstrate their commitment to their team members' well-being.

At the IT company, IBM, employees have access to a range of wellness programs, including mental health support, fitness classes, and healthy eating initiatives. This focus on employee well-being has led to increased job satisfaction, reduced turnover, and improved productivity.

**Conclusion**

Millennial managers have a unique opportunity to drive positive change in the workplace and create a culture that fosters growth, autonomy, and purpose. By implementing these five steps, leaders can create a work environment that benefits both the employee and the company, leading to increased job satisfaction, productivity, and retention. As millennials continue to move into management roles, it's important that they prioritize these strategies to create a workplace that is not only fulfilling but also sustainable for the long-term. By doing so, they can set an example for future generations of leaders and create a better future for work.

# ACHIEVING YOUR FULL POTENTIAL

# Chapter 17

---

## Finding Your Voice: Speaking Up When It Matters

In today's fast-paced and often polarized world, it can be challenging to speak up when we witness something ethically questionable, encounter offensive speech, or disagree with consensus opinion. According to a recent study, most people tend to remain silent in such situations, often rationalizing their inaction as a way to avoid conflict or maintain social harmony. However, as diligent employees, compassionate colleagues, and thoughtful leaders, it is crucial that we find the courage to lend our voices to the conversation.

In this chapter, we will explore the psychological challenges of speaking up, ways to lessen the social threat it creates, and practical strategies for making your voice heard.

## The Psychological Difficulty of Speaking Up

Speaking up when it matters can be a daunting task. It requires us to confront our fears of rejection, embarrassment, and social exclusion. Our brains are wired to avoid these negative outcomes, which can make it challenging to take the first step. According to Dr. Amy Edmondson, a renowned psychologist and author, "The fear of speaking up is not just about fear of conflict or disagreement, it's also about the fear of social exclusion."

Moreover, the pressure to conform to group norms can be overwhelming, making it easier to stay silent than to risk standing out. This is particularly true in situations where there is a strong consensus opinion, and dissenting voices are not welcome.

**Lessen the Social Threat**

To overcome the psychological barriers to speaking up, it's essential to create an environment where diverse perspectives are valued and respected. Leaders can play a crucial role in fostering such a culture by actively encouraging open communication and constructive criticism.

One effective way to lessen the social threat is to make it clear that you're not out to get anyone. Instead, your intention is to share your concerns or ideas to improve the situation or address a problem. This can be done by:

- Using "I" statements instead of "you" statements, which can come across as accusatory.

- Framing your concerns as questions rather than accusations.

- Avoiding inflammatory language and focusing on the issue at hand.

- Listening actively and responding thoughtfully to others' perspectives.

## Make an If-Then Plan

Creating an if-then plan can help you prepare for situations where you might need to speak up. This involves identifying potential scenarios where you would need to speak up and developing a plan of action for each one.

For instance, if you witness a colleague making an offensive comment, your if-then plan might include:

- Stating your concern directly and respectfully.

- Explaining how their comment affected you and why it's important to address.

- Offering a solution or suggestion for improvement.

Having a plan in place can help alleviate some of the anxiety associated with speaking up and increase the likelihood that you will take action when the time comes.

## Conclusion

Speaking up when it matters is never easy, but it's a crucial part of being a responsible and engaged member of society. By recognizing the psychological challenges that come with it, lessening the social threat, and creating an if-then plan, you can find the courage and confidence to make your voice heard. Remember, speaking up is not just about expressing your opinions; it's about creating a more inclusive, equitable, and just world for everyone. So, the next time you witness something ethically questionable, encounter offensive speech, or disagree with consensus opinion, don't be afraid to speak up. Your voice matters.

# ACHIEVING YOUR FULL POTENTIAL

# Chapter 18

## Developing Your Influence Skills: How to Effectively Persuade Others and Promote Your Ideas

Being able to influence others in a positive way is an important life and career skill. Whether trying to motivate team members at work or get buy-in for a new community initiative, the ability to effectively persuade others can help accomplish your goals. However, simply telling people what to do is rarely an effective influencing strategy. Gaining true influence requires understanding different perspectives, building trust with others, and crafting compelling arguments.

In this chapter, we will explore six key skills for strengthening your influence abilities based on research from leadership experts.

## Understanding Other Perspectives

The first step to influencing others is understanding perspectives different from your own. People are more open to new ideas when they feel heard and respected. As a leader, make time to listen without judgment and uncover what motivates different stakeholders. Ask open-ended questions to learn about others' priorities, experiences and potential concerns related to your proposals. Gathering these insights shows respect and will help tailor your arguments to be most convincing.

For example, during a staff meeting at a nonprofit, the director proposed launching two new outreach programs. However, when soliciting feedback, the accounting manager expressed worries about stretching existing budgets too thin. Rather than dismiss these concerns, the director had a private discussion to better understand the financial constraints. This led to modifying one program's scope and gaining the accountant's support for the revised plan.

**Building Rapport and Trust**

Earning influence requires building rapport with others over time through honest, empathetic interactions. People are more likely to accept ideas from those they know, like and trust. One effective strategy is finding common interests or values that can form a foundation for stronger professional relationships. Share relevant personal anecdotes to help colleagues see you as a multi-dimensional human being rather than just a coworker. Make eye contact, pay full attention during conversations, and remember key details people share to demonstrate your investment in their success too.

For example, a manager seeking a mentor built trust over lunches by discussing shared hobbies outside work like sports. Opening up in this way made their working relationship more collaborative long-term as invisible barriers broke down. It also set the stage for the mentee to later gain career advice and recommendation of an important new initiative.

**Coalition Building**

Rather than working alone, broaden your circle of influence by forming strategic alliances. Identify potential champions who could promote your ideas given their credibility with certain audiences. Provide value to coalition members by supporting their goals too so the relationship is a two-way partnership. For larger proposals, map stakeholder networks to target early adopters well-positioned to influence others. By enlisting these allies, momentum will build as proposals gain endorsements from respected colleagues.

For instance, a CEO gained advisory board approval for an acquisition by first briefing an advocate well-regarded in the medical research field. This supporter then quietly lobbied peers with complementary expertise to generate "grassroots" backing before the formal vote. With a critical mass of preliminary backing, naysayers found it harder to block the initiative.

**Framing Persuasive Arguments**

The effective framing and delivery of oral and written arguments is key to nudging others toward your perspective. Always define problems through the audiences' lenses by emphasizing impacts relevant to their priorities and values. Propose your solutions as reasonable next steps building on stakeholders' past interests or successful efforts. Support recommendations with compelling evidence and stories rather than heavy data alone. Tell a clear narrative customers and colleagues can easily envision becoming reality.

To convince investors in renewable energy, one startup emphasized job creation and energy independence instead of only returns. Their arguments resonated more given the times and caused term sheets to pile up as concerned stakeholders proactively sought involvement. By speaking audiences' language instead of their own, influence grew exponentially.

## Demonstrating Expertise

Nothing influences opinion like expertise relevant audiences respect. Consistently deliver accurate information and nuanced insights from your role at the forefront of trends, operations or team successes. Provide transparency into your working knowledge and efforts to benefit others. Over time, colleagues will perceive you as a valuable resource and come to respect the merits behind what you advocate.

A Lean coordinator at a factory steadily gained renown by hosting lunch-and-learn sessions covering tips gleaned from conferences. This allowed disseminating novel approaches and problem-solving strategies employees quickly incorporated into daily work. The coordinator's credibility expanded as suggested practices kept streamlining workflows and enhancing product quality. For future major initiatives, buy-in proved swift given a reservoir of goodwill.

**Gaining Commitments**

Once persuading stakeholders into agreement in principle, formalizing buy-in through written or verbal commitments activates feelings of consistency and completion vital for moving plans forward. Have interested parties state what support, resources or partnership they can offer to contribute to solutions discussed. Their promises help clarify expectations and accountability on both sides while motivating action through the psychology of consistency.

A PTO organized a school fundraiser more effectively by enabling preliminary pledges at initial kickoff meetings versus vague verbal assent alone. Public commitments by administrators to volunteer, promote on social media and approach local businesses generated concrete offerings that built enthusiasm and kept the campaign on track to exceed its goals.

**Conclusion**

Influence stems from a combination of interpersonal skills, expert knowledge and strategic alliances that take time to develop. By consistently applying techniques like relationship building, coalition formation and persuasive communication outlined above, any professional can strengthen their ability to lead positive change. True influence comes through mutual understanding and respect, not forceful directives. With practice, you'll gain colleagues' trust as a collaborator focused on jointly solving problems rather than pushing private agendas. Mastering influence paves the way to enacting solutions capable of meaningfully impacting organizations, communities and society as a whole.

ACHIEVING YOUR FULL POTENTIAL

# Chapter 19

# The Dangers of Workplace Enmeshment: How a Career Can Consume Your Identity and What to Do About It

In today's fast-paced, competitive job market, it's not uncommon for individuals to dedicate their entire lives to their careers. Many people strive for years to reach the top of their field, sacrificing time, energy, and personal relationships along the way. But what happens when your career becomes your whole identity? What happens when you lose yourself in your work and forget who you are outside of your job? This phenomenon is known as enmeshment, and it can lead to a painful identity crisis when the career you've dedicated your life to no longer exists.

In this chapter, we will explore the dangers of enmeshment and how to build a more balanced and robust identity.

**Enmeshment: A Loss of Personal Identity**

Enmeshment is a psychological phenomenon that occurs when the boundaries between individuals become unclear, and their identities become intertwined. In the context of a career, enmeshment happens when an individual's professional identity takes over their personal identity. This means that they become so closely identified with their job that their personal interests, values, and hobbies take a back seat.

Enmeshment can manifest in various ways. For instance, an individual may spend so much time at work that they have little time or energy left for personal pursuits. They may also feel pressure to conform to the expectations of their job, even if it means sacrificing their own beliefs and values. In extreme cases, enmeshment can lead to burnout, where an individual feels drained and disconnected from their personal life.

One of the main causes of enmeshment is societal pressure. In today's competitive job market, many people feel that they must dedicate themselves entirely to their work to succeed. This can lead to a culture of overwork and sacrifice, where individuals feel that their personal lives are secondary to their professional ones. Additionally, social media can exacerbate this issue by creating unrealistic expectations of success and achievement.

Another factor that contributes to enmeshment is the need for validation. Many people find their sense of self-worth through their work, and they may feel that their job is the most important aspect of their identity. This can make it difficult for them to disconnect from work and pursue personal interests, as they feel that their professional identity is at stake.

The consequences of enmeshment can be severe. It can lead to a loss of personal fulfillment, as individuals become disconnected from their passions and interests. Additionally, it can create a sense of isolation, as individuals become so focused on their work that they neglect their relationships with friends and family. In some cases, enmeshment can even lead to mental health issues such as anxiety and depression.

To avoid enmeshment, it's essential to strike a balance between work and personal life. This means setting boundaries around work hours and dedicating time to personal pursuits. It's also essential to explore one's interests and values outside of work, as this can help create a more well-rounded sense of identity. Additionally, employers can help prevent enmeshment by promoting a healthy work-life balance and creating a culture that values personal fulfillment.

**The Dangers of Enmeshment**

When your career becomes your whole identity, you become vulnerable to a range of negative emotions and experiences. Burnout, layoffs, and retirement can lead to a painful identity crisis, as you struggle to come to terms with who you are outside of your job. Individuals in these situations frequently suffer from anxiety, depression, and despair.

- *Burnout*: When your career is your entire identity, it's easy to become consumed by work-related stress. Long hours, high expectations, and constant pressure can lead to physical and mental exhaustion. Burnout can cause individuals to feel unfulfilled, unhappy, and unmotivated, leading to a crisis of identity.

- *Layoffs*: Suddenly losing your job can be a devastating blow to your identity. When your career is your whole identity, it's difficult to separate your professional and personal self. A layoff can lead to feelings of failure, inadequacy, and a loss of purpose.

- *Retirement*: Retirement can be a challenging time for individuals who have dedicated their entire lives to their careers. Without a job to define them, they may struggle to find meaning and purpose in their lives.

## Building a Balanced Identity

The key to avoiding the dangers of enmeshment is to build a more balanced and robust identity. This involves diversifying your activities and relationships, and claiming back some time for yourself. Here are some ways to do this:

- *Pursue Hobbies and Interests*: Make time for activities that bring you joy and fulfillment outside of work. Whether it's painting, playing music, or hiking, hobbies can help you develop a sense of purpose and identity that's not tied to your job.

- *Nurture Personal Relationships*: Build strong relationships with family and friends that are not based on your professional identity. This can help you maintain a sense of self-worth and belonging outside of your career.

- *Take Time for Self-Reflection*: Take time to reflect on your values, interests, and goals. Identify what's important to you, and make sure your career aligns with these values.

- *Develop a Growth Mindset*: Embrace the idea that you are not fixed and can always learn and grow. Developing a growth mindset can help you see your career as a journey, rather than a fixed identity.

## Conclusion

Enmeshment can lead to a painful identity crisis when your career no longer exists. To avoid this, it's essential to build a more balanced and robust identity that's not solely defined by your job. By pursuing hobbies and interests, nurturing personal relationships, taking time for self-reflection, and developing a growth mindset, you can create a fulfilling life outside of your career. Remember, your career is a part of your life, but it's not your whole identity.

In conclusion, building a balanced and robust identity requires effort and dedication, but it's worth it in the long run. By taking steps to diversify your activities and relationships, and claiming back some time for yourself, you can avoid the dangers of enmeshment and maintain a healthy, fulfilling life both in and outside of your career.

ACHIEVING YOUR FULL POTENTIAL

… ACHIEVING YOUR FULL POTENTIAL

# ACHIEVING YOUR FULL POTENTIAL

# Part 5

# Change Management and Adaptability

ACHIEVING YOUR FULL POTENTIAL

# Chapter 20

## Adapting to Change: The Four Attributes of Successful Learners

In today's business environment, the ability to adapt and learn new skills is crucial for executives who want to stay ahead of the curve. With the constant shifts in how businesses operate and how work must get done, it's no longer enough to rely on traditional methods and approaches. To succeed, executives must be willing to experiment, take risks, and become novices over and over again. But this can be a challenging proposition, especially for those who are used to relying on their innate biases and established ways of doing things.

In this chapter, we will explore the four key attributes that successful learners possess, and how they can be developed through simple mental strategies. By cultivating these attributes, executives can better navigate the ever-changing landscape of modern business and stay ahead of the competition.

## Aspiration: The Desire to Learn and Master New Skills

The first attribute of successful learners is aspiration, or the desire to understand and master new skills. This involves having a growth mindset, being open to new experiences, and setting clear goals for personal and professional development. Aspiration is what drives individuals to push beyond their comfort zones and embrace new challenges.

One way to develop aspiration is to set "stretch goals" that are slightly beyond your current capabilities. By setting goals that are challenging but achievable, you'll be motivated to learn and grow, without feeling overwhelmed or discouraged. Additionally, seeking out mentors or coaches who can provide guidance and support can help you stay on track and overcome obstacles.

## Self-Awareness: Seeing Yourself Clearly

The second attribute of successful learners is self-awareness, or the ability to see oneself clearly. This involves being honest with yourself about your strengths and weaknesses, and understanding how your thoughts, feelings, and behaviors impact your learning and performance. Self-awareness allows individuals to identify areas for improvement and develop strategies for addressing them.

One way to develop self-awareness is to regularly reflect on your experiences and feedback from others. This can involve journaling, meditation, or seeking feedback from colleagues and mentors. By taking the time to reflect on your thoughts, feelings, and actions, you'll gain a better understanding of yourself and your learning processes, and be able to make adjustments as needed.

## Curiosity: Thinking of and Asking Good Questions

The third attribute of successful learners is curiosity, or the desire to learn and understand new things. This involves asking questions, seeking out new experiences, and being open to alternative perspectives. Curiosity is what drives individuals to explore new ideas and approaches, and to challenge their existing beliefs and assumptions.

One way to develop curiosity is to ask "why" and "what if" questions. By asking questions that challenge your assumptions and explore different possibilities, you'll gain a deeper understanding of the world around you and identify new opportunities for growth and learning. Additionally, seeking out diverse perspectives and experiences can help you broaden your horizons and develop a more nuanced understanding of the world.

## Vulnerability: Tolerating Mistakes and Learning from Failure

The fourth and final attribute of successful learners is vulnerability, or the willingness to take risks and tolerate mistakes. This involves being open to new experiences and perspectives, even if they challenge your existing beliefs and approaches. Vulnerability allows individuals to learn from their mistakes and use them as opportunities for growth and development.

One way to develop vulnerability is to embrace a "growth mindset" and view mistakes as opportunities for learning. By reframing failures as opportunities for growth, you'll be more likely to take risks and experiment with new approaches. Additionally, seeking out feedback and constructive criticism can help you identify areas for improvement and develop strategies for addressing them.

## Conclusion

In today's rapidly changing business environment, the ability to adapt and learn new skills is crucial for executives who want to stay ahead of the curve. By cultivating the four attributes of successful learners – aspiration, self-awareness, curiosity, and vulnerability – executives can better navigate the ever-changing landscape of modern business and stay ahead of the competition. While these attributes may seem daunting, they can be developed through simple mental strategies and practices.

# ACHIEVING YOUR FULL POTENTIAL

# Chapter 21

## Change Management: Navigating the Turbulent Waters of Organizational Change

Change in life is inevitable, and this extends to every transformational project undertaken by a corporation. Whether it's a system implementation, digital transformation, merger/acquisition, or post-COVID return-to-the-office push, change is ever-present and undeniably challenging. In making his case for a seismic shift, a character on the award-winning series Ted Lasso noted:

"In the beginning some people will hate this because some people hate change. But remember – at one time we only rode horses and hated the idea of automobiles. Now we can't live without our cars, and the hot dogs you just ate are 85% horse meat. Change is inevitable."

While I can't speak to the nutritional content of hot dogs, I do take issue with the notion that some people hate change. I'd argue that most people in fact hate change. Routines are comfortable, and changes to a routine are often an uncomfortable disruption. So how do we effectively manage change and ensure the desired outcomes are achieved? Read on for some tips on successfully navigating organizational change.

## Focus on the Benefits

The easiest was to engender early buy-in for organizational change is to address the critical question of "What's in it for me?" (WIIFM) for those whose way of working will be directly impacted. Oftentimes corporations offer loose rationale for change that doesn't resonate with their employees. Vague statements about a coming change, such that it is based on a strategic corporate initiative, that it will improve the bottom line, or even that it will make everyone's job easier, will not move the needle for most folks when it comes to their appetite for change. Instead, offer concrete statements about how the new process will benefit the individual employee. The "WIIFM" need not be colossal, but it must illustrate some personal benefit to your workforce. "The increased efficiency from this new process will free up one hour each Friday for you to plan for the coming week," or "We'll allocate a portion of the savings expected from this upgrade to replacing the coffee machines in the break room with newer models" will go a long way.

## Communicate with Clarity and Empathy

Organizational change inevitably affects the way people within the firm perform their jobs, which can lead to a sense of uncertainty and anxiety. It's critical that companies have open channels of communication to build trust, reassure employees, and educate them about the coming change.

Keep these pointers in mind to ensure effective communication over the life of the change:

- *Start early.* It's never too early to start socializing a coming change. The more time employees have to adjust to the idea of the new environment, and to ask questions about the coming change, the better.

- *Be clear and concise.* Employees need to understand why the change is necessary, how the change will impact them personally, and how the change will benefit both themselves individually and the company as a whole.

- *Be honest and transparent.* Employees won't expect to know every detail of a coming change, but they will assume that they can trust the information that is provided to them. Be forthright with what you share, making sure not to sugar-coat details; if asked about specifics you're not yet ready to divulge, feel comfortable noting that these details are still being finalized.

- *Reach all employees.* Targeted email blasts can be an effective method of providing updates on the change, but what about those employees who work on the manufacturing floor and may not have access to corporate email? Employ a variety of methods – emails, posters, manager-led stand-ups, fireside chats, even branded t-shirts – to share messaging on the change.

- *Be empathetic.* From the CEO to the front-line workers, change is challenging for everyone. Show patience and understand that everyone adjusts to change on their own timeline.

## Recognize that One Size Does Not Fit All

It is essential to adapt your change management approach to align with different work environments. For remote or hybrid teams, leveraging virtual tools such as a Digital Learning Platform (DLP) can be effective. While testimonials and webinars can help convey messages to a digitally connected audience, employing low-tech tools like signage, t-shirts, and face-to-face interactions will help drive acceptance of change among those workers with less tech access.

In addition to different work environments, effective change management considers the company's size, history with change, and unique characteristics. Our recommendations for the same ERP implementation would be significantly different for an emerging tech start-up than for a mid-market manufacturer or a franchise with multiple outposts. The key is having an agile mindset and tailoring the change management approach to each situation.

## Culture is Key

One of the most important factors to consider when managing change is company culture. People like to think they can quickly change a corporation's culture. Spoiler alert – you can't! The tone and approach you apply to your communications and training will vary from one company to another based on their norms and ways of working. Rather than trying to bend a company's culture to conform to a formulaic change approach, embrace the working environment and adjust your strategy to increase engagement and ensure a smooth transition.

Regardless of the initiative, be it an ERP implementation or a corporate reorganization, successful change requires a holistic approach that addresses the cultural needs of the organization. In addition to the typical stakeholder and impact assessments that are often conducted at the beginning of a change initiative, it's a great idea to deploy a culture assessment, which will set a baseline and underpin the entire change strategy.

**Celebrate Successes**

As the change initiative progresses, be sure to celebrate the little wins. Establish clear goals at the start of your change initiative and identify corresponding milestones. When you reach these key project points, pause and recognize everyone's efforts. A little thanks goes a long way in keeping groups motivated and maintaining engagement. Order lunch in for the team, treat them to happy hour, or let them sign off a couple hours early on a Friday afternoon to show your appreciation.

## ACHIEVING YOUR FULL POTENTIAL

None of us can escape change, but we can adapt how we respond to and embrace new norms. Employing the tips discussed herein will increase your chances of successfully ushering in change, deepen team cohesiveness, and lay the groundwork for a future of successful change at your organization.

ACHIEVING YOUR FULL POTENTIAL

# Chapter 22

## The Power of "How": Transforming Our Approach to Problem-Solving

As children, we learned to ask "Why?" and "Why not?" to understand the world around us. This curiosity is essential for learning and growth, but as we become adults and managers, this instinct can actually hinder our effectiveness. We often find ourselves stuck in "back-to-front" conversations, focusing on understanding the reasons behind a problem rather than finding solutions.

In this chapter, we will explore the benefits of replacing "Why?" with "How?" and adopting a forward-looking approach to problem-solving.

**The Limitations of "Why?"**

"Why?" is a natural question that helps us uncover the root cause of a problem. However, when we rely solely on this question, we can get stuck in a cycle of analysis paralysis. We may spend hours discussing the reasons behind a problem, trying to understand every detail, without actually finding a solution. This approach can lead to frustration and inaction, as we become mired in the past instead of moving towards the future.

For example, imagine a team leader who is struggling to meet project deadlines. They might ask, "Why are we always missing our deadlines?" The team might respond with a variety of reasons, such as lack of resources, poor communication, or inadequate planning. While these reasons are valid, they don't offer a clear path forward. The conversation might continue, with the leader asking, "Why didn't we plan better?" or "Why don't we have enough resources?" and so on. This cycle of questioning can continue indefinitely, leaving the team feeling unproductive and unfocused.

**The Power of "How?"**

In contrast, asking "How?" shifts the conversation towards solutions and action. Instead of dwelling on the past, "How?" allows us to explore ways to address the problem and move forward. This question encourages creativity, innovation, and collaboration. By asking "How?" we can identify practical steps to overcome challenges and achieve our goals.

To continue the previous example, instead of asking "Why are we always missing our deadlines?" the team leader could ask, "How can we plan better for our next project?" or "How can we allocate resources more effectively?" These questions promote discussion and brainstorming, focusing the team's energy on finding solutions rather than dwelling on past mistakes.

**The Benefits of a Forward-Looking Approach**

Adopting a forward-looking approach by asking "How?" has several advantages:

a. *Fosters Creativity*: By focusing on the future, we open ourselves up to new ideas and possibilities. Instead of being limited by past experiences, we can explore innovative solutions that might not have been considered otherwise.

b. *Encourages Collaboration*: When we ask "How?" we invite others to contribute their ideas and insights. This collaborative approach builds trust and promotes a sense of shared ownership in finding solutions.

c. *Increases Efficiency*: By focusing on practical steps, we can streamline our problem-solving process and reduce the risk of getting bogged down in lengthy discussions. This approach helps us identify the most effective actions to address the problem at hand.

d. *Reduces Stress and Frustration*: The "How?" approach emphasizes action and progress, which can help reduce stress and frustration. When we feel overwhelmed by a problem, asking "How?" can help us break it down into manageable tasks, making it feel less daunting.

## Overcoming the Fear of Change

While the benefits of asking "How?" are numerous, some people may resist this approach. They might feel uncomfortable abandoning the familiar "Why?" or worry that they'll miss out on understanding the root cause of the problem. However, it's important to remember that understanding the reasons behind a problem is not always necessary to find a solution. In many cases, the root cause may not be readily apparent, and even if it were, understanding it might not lead to a clear path forward.

To overcome this fear, it's essential to recognize that "How?" is not a replacement for "Why?" but rather a complementary approach. We can still ask "Why?" when it's appropriate, but we should balance it with "How?" to ensure we're focusing on solutions as well as understanding.

## Conclusion

The way we approach problem-solving can significantly impact our effectiveness as managers and leaders. By replacing "Why?" with "How?" we can shift our focus from the past to the future, foster creativity, encourage collaboration, increase efficiency, and reduce stress and frustration. While understanding the root cause of a problem is important, it's not always necessary to find a solution. By embracing the power of "How?" we can unlock new possibilities and create a more productive, forward-thinking work environment. So the next time you're faced with a challenge, try asking "How?" instead of "Why?" and watch your team's problem-solving skills flourish.

ACHIEVING YOUR FULL POTENTIAL

# Chapter 23

## The Performance Management Revolution: Moving Away from Traditional Appraisals

The traditional performance appraisal process has been a staple of organizational life for decades, but it has been widely criticized for its limitations and ineffectiveness. In recent years, more than a third of U.S. companies have abandoned traditional performance appraisals in favor of a more modern and development-focused approach.

In this chapter, we will explore the reasons behind this shift and the alternative approaches that organizations are adopting.

## Evolution of Performance Management

Performance management has undergone significant changes over the years. In the past, the primary focus was on evaluating employee performance to determine compensation and promotions. However, as the labor market has tightened and the business environment has become more rapidly changing, organizations have come to realize that traditional performance appraisals are no longer effective in meeting their needs.

## The Limitations of Traditional Performance Appraisals

Traditional performance appraisals have several limitations that have led to their decline in popularity. Firstly, they focus primarily on holding employees accountable for their past performance, rather than improving their future performance. This creates a culture of blame and criticism, rather than one of development and improvement. Secondly, traditional appraisals are often seen as a necessary evil, rather than a valuable tool for employee growth and development. Finally, they can create a sense of competition among employees, rather than fostering a collaborative team environment.

## The Benefits of Development-Focused Conversations

In contrast to traditional performance appraisals, development-focused conversations offer several benefits. Firstly, they allow managers and employees to have regular, open conversations about performance, rather than waiting for an annual review. This enables employees to receive feedback and make adjustments in real-time, rather than waiting for a year-end review. Secondly, these conversations focus on improving employee performance, rather than simply evaluating it. This creates a culture of continuous improvement and development, rather than one of criticism and accountability. Finally, development-focused conversations promote teamwork and collaboration, rather than competition among employees.

## Hybrid Approaches to Performance Management

Some organizations are hesitant to abandon traditional performance appraisals entirely, and are instead adopting hybrid approaches that combine elements of traditional appraisals with development-focused conversations. For example, some companies are giving employees performance ratings on multiple dimensions, coupled with regular development feedback. This allows employees to receive feedback on their performance, while also having regular conversations about their development and growth.

## Addressing Concerns about Goal Alignment, Merit Raises, and Discrimination

One of the concerns about moving away from traditional performance appraisals is that it may be harder to align individual and organizational goals, award merit raises, identify poor performers, and counter claims of discrimination. However, traditional appraisals have not been effective in addressing these issues either. Instead, organizations are finding that development-focused conversations and hybrid approaches can actually help to address these concerns more effectively. For example, by having regular conversations about performance and development, managers can better align employee goals with organizational objectives. Additionally, merit raises can be based on employee performance and development, rather than simply on past performance. Finally, development-focused conversations can help to identify areas where employees may need additional support or training, rather than simply labeling them as poor performers.

## Conclusion

The traditional performance appraisal process has been criticized for its limitations and ineffectiveness. In response, organizations are moving towards more development-focused conversations between managers and employees. These conversations promote a culture of continuous improvement and teamwork, rather than criticism and competition. While there are concerns about abandoning traditional appraisals, hybrid approaches and development-focused conversations can actually help to address these concerns more effectively. As the labor market continues to tighten and the business environment continues to change, it is likely that the performance management revolution will continue to gain momentum.

ACHIEVING YOUR FULL POTENTIAL

# Chapter 24

# Empowering Employees to Go Beyond Their Jobs: The Art of Citizenship Crafting

In today's competitive business landscape, organizations need employees who are not only productive but also willing to go the extra mile. Research has shown that employees who engage in extra-role behaviors, also known as "citizenship behaviors," contribute significantly to their company's efficiency and effectiveness. These behaviors include helping out coworkers, volunteering for special assignments, introducing new ideas and work practices, attending non-mandatory meetings, and putting in extra hours to complete important projects.

However, it's not enough to simply expect employees to exhibit these behaviors. Managers must take an active role in motivating their team members to engage in citizenship behaviors. One effective way to do this is through a concept called "citizenship crafting," which involves redesigning work to play to employees' strengths, motives, and passions.

In this chapter, we will explore the concept of citizenship crafting and provide specific examples of how managers can empower their employees to go beyond their jobs.

## Task Crafting

Task crafting involves altering aspects of the job itself to make it more engaging and meaningful for employees. Managers can do this by giving employees the autonomy to choose their own projects, allowing them to work on tasks that align with their interests and strengths. For example, a marketing manager could give their team members the freedom to choose the social media platforms they want to focus on, or a software development team leader could allow their team to choose the features they want to add to their product.

Another way to implement task crafting is by providing opportunities for employees to learn new skills and take on new challenges. This not only helps employees feel more engaged but also helps the organization as a whole by developing a more skilled workforce. For instance, a financial analyst could be given the opportunity to learn data analysis and visualization tools, or a customer service representative could be trained in conflict resolution techniques.

## Relationship Crafting

Relationship crafting involves altering the people with whom employees work to create a more supportive and collaborative work environment. Managers can do this by fostering open communication, encouraging teamwork, and creating opportunities for employees to build meaningful relationships with their colleagues. For example, a manager could create cross-functional teams to work on projects, allowing employees to collaborate with people from different departments and build new relationships.

Managers can also encourage mentorship programs, where experienced employees can guide and support less experienced colleagues. This not only helps employees feel more connected but also helps to develop their skills and knowledge. For instance, a senior software engineer could mentor a junior developer, providing guidance and feedback on their code and helping them to improve their skills.

**Cognitive Crafting**

Cognitive crafting involves altering employees' mindset about their jobs to make them more meaningful and engaging. Managers can do this by helping employees see the bigger picture and understand how their work contributes to the organization's overall goals. For example, a manager could provide regular updates on the company's progress and achievements, highlighting the impact that employees' work has on the business.

Another way to implement cognitive crafting is by encouraging employees to think creatively and suggest new ideas and work practices. This not only helps employees feel more engaged but also helps the organization innovate and stay ahead of the competition. For instance, a manager could hold regular brainstorming sessions, where employees are encouraged to share their ideas and suggestions for improving processes and procedures.

## Conclusion

Citizenship crafting is a powerful tool that managers can use to motivate employees to go beyond their jobs and engage in extra-role behaviors. By redesigning work to play to employees' strengths, motives, and passions, managers can create a more engaged, productive, and innovative workforce. The three aspects of citizenship crafting - task crafting, relationship crafting, and cognitive crafting - provide managers with practical ways to empower their employees and make work more meaningful and less depleting.

By implementing citizenship crafting, managers can not only improve their employees' well-being but also contribute to their organization's success. As a result, it's essential for managers to understand the concept of citizenship crafting and start implementing it in their workplace. By doing so, they'll not only create a more positive work environment but also empower their people and encourage continual growth and development.

# ACHIEVING YOUR FULL POTENTIAL

# ACHIEVING YOUR FULL POTENTIAL

… ACHIEVING YOUR FULL POTENTIAL

# Part 6

# Personal Leadership Development

ACHIEVING YOUR FULL POTENTIAL

# Chapter 25

## The Power of Untouchable Days: Protecting Your Creative Flow

In today's fast-paced, constantly connected world, it's easy to get sucked into a never-ending cycle of meetings, emails, and distractions. For creative professionals, this can be particularly detrimental to productivity and flow. That's why the concept of "Untouchable Days" is becoming increasingly popular.

In this chapter, we will explore the benefits of scheduling "untouchable days", how to make them work for you, and what to do when unexpected opportunities or obligations arise.

**What are Untouchable Days?**

Untouchable Days are days set aside for deep, uninterrupted work. They are sacred, untouchable blocks of time where nothing can interrupt you – no texts, no emails, no phone calls, and absolutely no meetings. The idea is to create a protected space for creative work, free from distractions and interruptions.

The benefits of untouchable days include:

1. *Increased Productivity*: By dedicating a full day to uninterrupted work, you can achieve a state of flow, which is essential for high-quality creative output. Research shows that working in uninterrupted 90-120 minute increments, followed by short breaks, can increase productivity and improve work-life balance.

2. *Improved Focus*: Untouchable Days help you maintain focus on your most important tasks. Interruptions can derail your train of thought, causing you to lose valuable time and mental energy. By eliminating distractions, you can sustain your focus and work at your best.

3. *Better Work-Life Balance*: Scheduling Untouchable Days allows you to prioritize your personal and professional life. By dedicating one day a week to deep work, you can avoid the stress and burnout that come with constantly juggling tasks and responsibilities.

4. *Enhanced Creativity*: Untouchable Days provide the space and time to explore new ideas and approaches. Without the pressure of meetings and deadlines, you can let your mind wander, experiment, and innovate, leading to better work and personal growth.

## Making Untouchable Days Work for You

1. *Schedule Them in Advance*: To make Untouchable Days effective, schedule them in advance and treat them as non-negotiable. Mark them on your calendar like you would any other important appointment or commitment.

2. *Communicate with Your Team and Clients*: Let your team and clients know that you have Untouchable Days and that you're unavailable during those times. Set clear expectations and establish a system for emergencies.

3. *Be Flexible*: While Untouchable Days are meant to be sacrosanct, unexpected opportunities or obligations may arise. Don't be too rigid – if something truly important comes up, consider moving your Untouchable Day to another day that week. However, avoid moving it to a different week altogether, as this can disrupt your creative flow and undermine the benefits of the Untouchable Day.

4. *Make the Most of Your Untouchable Day*: Use your Untouchable Day wisely. Prepare for it by setting clear goals, eliminating distractions, and creating an environment conducive to focus. Take breaks, practice self-care, and refuel to maintain your energy and productivity.

## How to Prepare for an Untouchable Day and Set Clear Goals

Preparing for an Untouchable Day requires careful planning and deliberate goal-setting. Here are some tips to help you make the most of your Untouchable Day:

1. *Prepare a plan of action*: Before your Untouchable Day, take some time to reflect on your goals and priorities. Identify the most important tasks that require your undivided attention, and create a plan of action for tackling them. Be specific about what you want to achieve and how you'll go about it.

2. *Eliminate distractions*: Make sure your workspace is conducive to focus and creativity. Turn off notifications, log out of social media, and eliminate any other distractions that might interrupt your flow. Consider using tools like website blockers or apps that help you stay focused.

3. *Set realistic goals*: Be realistic about what you can achieve in a day. Don't overload yourself with too many tasks, as this can lead to burnout and decreased productivity. Prioritize your most important tasks and focus on delivering quality work rather than quantity.

4. *Take breaks*: Remember to take breaks throughout the day to recharge and refuel. Schedule breaks into your plan of action, and use them to do something that energizes you, like going for a walk, practicing yoga, or reading a book.

5. *Practice self-care*: Untouchable Days can be intense, so make sure you're taking care of yourself. Stay hydrated, eat nutritious food, and get enough sleep. Avoid overworking yourself, and take time to relax and unwind when your work is done.

By following these tips, you'll be well on your way to a productive and fulfilling Untouchable Day. Remember, the key is to be deliberate with your time and focus on delivering high-quality work.

## Conclusion

Untouchable days are a powerful tool for creative professionals looking to enhance their productivity, focus, and work-life balance. By dedicating one day a week to uninterrupted work, you can achieve a state of flow, improve your creativity, and maintain a healthy balance between work and personal life. Remember to schedule them in advance, communicate with your team and clients, be flexible, and make the most of your

Untouchable Day. Embrace the concept of Untouchable Days and watch your creative output soar!

ACHIEVING YOUR FULL POTENTIAL

# Chapter 26

## The Art of Letting Go: Shifting from Ego-Drive to Co-Drive Leadership

As leaders, we often start our careers with a strong focus on speed and energy. We strive to achieve more, faster, and better than anyone else. We rely on our "ego-drive" to propel us forward and make a name for ourselves. However, as we progress in our careers, we come to realize that there's a limit to how much we can achieve alone. We need to rely on others, to work with them, and to empower them to achieve their full potential. This shift from ego-drive to co-drive leadership is a crucial step in our professional growth and development.

In this chapter, we will explore the main points of this transition and provide specific examples to help you understand and implement them in your own leadership journey.

**From Energetic to Energizing**

As leaders, we often start out as energetic and charismatic individuals who set the pace for our teams. We work tirelessly to inspire and motivate our colleagues, often relying on our own energy and enthusiasm to drive results. However, as we move towards co-drive leadership, we need to shift our focus from being energetic to being energizing. Instead of being the source of energy, we need to create an environment where our team members can generate their own energy and motivation.

For example, a CEO of a startup might start out by being the driving force behind the company's vision and strategy. However, as the company grows, they need to transition from being the sole energizer to empowering their team members to take ownership of their work and drive their own initiatives. This can be achieved by providing opportunities for professional development, encouraging collaboration, and recognizing and celebrating individual and team achievements.

## From Delegating to Allowing Congregation

As leaders, we often delegate tasks to our team members, expecting them to execute them to the best of their abilities. However, as we transition to co-drive leadership, we need to move away from delegating and towards allowing congregation. Instead of dictating tasks, we need to create an environment where our team members can come together, share ideas, and collaborate on projects.

For example, a manager of a marketing team might start out by assigning specific tasks to each team member. However, as they transition to co-drive leadership, they might create cross-functional teams that work together to develop marketing campaigns. They might also encourage team members to share their ideas and collaborate on projects, rather than simply following orders.

## From Pushing Harder to Letting Go

As leaders, we often focus on pushing ourselves and our teams harder to achieve better results. However, as we transition to co-drive leadership, we need to shift our focus from pushing harder to letting go. Instead of trying to control every aspect of our work, we need to trust our team members to take ownership of their work and empower them to make decisions.

For example, a project manager might start out by micromanaging every aspect of a project. However, as they transition to co-drive leadership, they might focus on providing guidance and support, rather than trying to control every detail. They might also empower their team members to make decisions and take ownership of their work, rather than needing to approve every step of the way.

## Creating an Environment that Allows for Congregation and Collaboration Among Team Members

Creating an environment that fosters congregation and collaboration among team members is an excellent way to promote growth, innovation, and productivity within an organization.

First and foremost, leaders must establish a culture of trust and respect. Team members must feel comfortable sharing their ideas and opinions without fear of reprisal or ridicule. Leaders can facilitate this by being approachable, open-minded, and receptive to feedback.

Secondly, leaders must encourage communication and the sharing of ideas. This can be achieved through regular team meetings, brainstorming sessions, and casual gatherings. Leaders should also consider implementing an open-door policy, where team members can drop by their office at any time to discuss their thoughts and ideas.

Thirdly, leaders must provide opportunities for team members to work together on projects. This can be done by creating cross-functional teams, hosting workshops, and organizing team-building activities. By working together, team members can learn from one another, build relationships, and develop a sense of camaraderie.

Fourthly, leaders must embrace diversity and inclusivity. A diverse and inclusive workplace fosters a sense of belonging, which in turn promotes collaboration and teamwork. Leaders should strive to create a work environment that is welcoming and accepting of all employees, regardless of their background, race, gender, or sexual orientation.

Lastly, leaders must lead by example. They must demonstrate the behaviors and attitudes they wish to see in their team members. By being approachable, collaborative, and open-minded, leaders can inspire their team members to do the same.

Creating an environment that fosters congregation and collaboration among team members requires a combination of trust, communication, opportunity, diversity, and leadership by example. By following these principles, leaders can create a workplace where team members feel valued, motivated, and empowered to achieve their full potential.

## Conclusion

Shifting from ego-drive to co-drive leadership is a crucial step in our professional growth and development. By moving away from relying solely on our own energy and enthusiasm and towards empowering our team members, we can achieve greater results and create a more collaborative and motivated work environment. It's not an easy transition, but with practice, patience, and a willingness to let go, we can become more effective leaders who inspire and empower others to achieve their full potential.

# ACHIEVING YOUR FULL POTENTIAL

# ACHIEVING YOUR FULL POTENTIAL

# Chapter 27

## The Power of Soft Skills: Unlocking Success in the Workplace

In today's evolving and interconnected world, the importance of soft skills cannot be underestimated. While technical expertise and hard skills are undoubtedly essential, it is the soft skills that truly set individuals apart and drive success in the workplace. Soft skills encompass a range of interpersonal, communication, and emotional intelligence abilities that enable individuals to effectively navigate complex situations, build strong relationships, and lead with impact.

In this chapter, we will explore the power of soft skills and provide specific examples to highlight their significance in personal and professional growth.

**Emotional Intelligence: The Foundation of Soft Skills**

*Understanding and Managing Emotions:* Emotional intelligence is a crucial component of soft skills, allowing individuals to understand and manage their emotions effectively. This skill enables leaders to maintain composure in challenging situations, empathize with others, and make thoughtful decisions. For instance, a leader who possesses emotional intelligence can diffuse conflicts by understanding the underlying emotions and finding common ground for resolution.

*Building Strong Relationships:* Soft skills such as empathy, active listening, and effective communication foster strong relationships in the workplace. By actively listening and showing empathy, leaders can create an environment where employees feel valued and understood. This leads to increased collaboration, trust, and productivity within teams, ultimately driving organizational success.

## Communication Skills: The Bridge to Success

*Clear and Effective Communication:* Clear and effective communication is a hallmark of successful leaders. Soft skills like active listening, clarity, and adaptability in communication enable leaders to convey their ideas, expectations, and feedback in a way that is easily understood by others. Through effective communication, leaders can align their team towards a common goal and foster a culture of open dialogue.

*Conflict Resolution:* Conflict is inevitable within any organization, but leaders with strong soft skills can navigate and resolve conflicts with finesse. By actively listening to different perspectives, understanding the underlying issues, and communicating diplomatically, leaders can find win-win solutions that bring about positive change and maintain harmonious working relationships.

## Leadership and Collaboration: Driving Organizational Success

*Inspiring and Motivating Others:* Leaders with strong soft skills have the ability to inspire and motivate their teams towards achieving shared goals. By demonstrating empathy, showing appreciation for their team's efforts, and providing constructive feedback, leaders can create a positive work environment that fosters growth, innovation, and high performance.

*Collaboration and Team Building:* Effective collaboration is a key driver of success in today's interconnected world. Soft skills such as teamwork, adaptability, and conflict management enable leaders to build cohesive teams that thrive on diverse perspectives and skills. Through collaboration, leaders can leverage the strengths of each team member, leading to enhanced problem-solving capabilities and greater innovation.

**Conclusion**

The power of soft skills cannot be underestimated in today's rapidly evolving workplace. Emotional intelligence, communication skills, and leadership abilities are at the heart of soft skills, enabling individuals to navigate complex situations, build strong relationships, and drive organizational success. By developing and honing these skills, individuals can unlock their true potential and excel in their personal and professional lives. As leaders, let us recognize the significance of soft skills and strive to cultivate them within ourselves and our teams for a brighter future.

# ACHIEVING YOUR FULL POTENTIAL

ACHIEVING YOUR FULL POTENTIAL

# Chapter 28

## Investing in Self-Awareness and Accountability: Mastering Foundational Capabilities for Team Success

Building a high-performing team requires more than just focusing on the collective dynamics. It necessitates individual self-reflection and personal growth. When a team is not functioning optimally, it is crucial to recognize that each team member, including the leader, plays a role in contributing to the challenges. To enhance the team's dynamic in a meaningful and sustainable way, it is essential for everyone to cultivate three foundational capabilities: internal self-awareness, external self-awareness, and personal accountability.

In this chapter, we will delve into these capabilities and provide specific examples to illustrate their significance.

## Internal Self-Awareness: Understanding Your Impact

Internal self-awareness is the cornerstone of personal growth and effective team functioning. It involves recognizing and comprehending one's feelings, beliefs, and values, and how they shape one's reactions. When faced with emotionally charged situations, it is vital to pause and reflect. Ask yourself questions such as:

1. *Core Values and Reactions*: What are my core values, and how might they be influencing my reactions in this situation? By examining how your values align or conflict with the circumstances, you can gain clarity on your emotional responses.

2. *Facts vs. Interpretations*: Differentiating between facts and interpretations is crucial. Ask yourself, "What are the objective facts in this situation, and what are my subjective interpretations?" This introspection enables

you to approach the situation with a more objective mindset, reducing the potential for biased reactions.

## External Self-Awareness: Observing and Seeking Feedback

External self-awareness involves understanding the impact you have on your teammates and the team as a whole. By observing their behaviors and seeking their feedback, you can gain valuable insights into how you are perceived and how your actions influence team dynamics.

1. *Observational Awareness*: During team discussions, be attentive to non-verbal cues and behaviors exhibited by your teammates. Did someone raise their voice, stop talking, or smile? These observations can provide valuable information about their reactions and engagement levels. However, it is important to note that these observations may be subject to misinterpretation.

2. *Feedback-seeking Approach*: A more direct and effective approach to enhancing external self-awareness is to actively seek specific feedback from your teammates. Ask them questions such as: "What am I doing in meetings that is helpful?" and "What am I doing that is not helpful?" This direct feedback allows you to gain a

clearer understanding of how your actions impact the team and identify areas for improvement.

## Personal Accountability: Assessing and Adapting

Personal accountability is a crucial capability for improving team outcomes. It involves taking ownership of one's contribution to the team's challenges and consciously choosing how to respond to enhance the team's performance.

1. *Assessing Your Contribution*: Practice self-reflection and assess how your behaviors and actions contribute to the identified team challenges. By acknowledging your role in the problem, you can take proactive steps towards finding solutions.

2. *Making Conscious Choices*: Once you have identified your contribution, make a conscious choice about how to react to improve the team's outcomes. This may involve adapting your communication style, seeking support from colleagues, or taking on additional responsibilities. The key is to actively participate in the resolution process and demonstrate your commitment to positive change.

## Conclusion

To improve team dynamics and foster a high-performing team, it is essential to start with self-improvement. By mastering the foundational capabilities of internal self-awareness, external self-awareness, and personal accountability, you can create a positive impact on team dynamics. Remember that change requires both learning and consistent practice to form new habits. By continuously honing these capabilities, you will not only improve your own effectiveness as a team member or leader but also inspire others to follow suit. Embrace the opportunity for personal growth, and watch as your team flourishes.

ACHIEVING YOUR FULL POTENTIAL

# Chapter 29

## Striking the Balance: Sharing Your Authentic Self at Work

In today's professional landscape, the concept of bringing one's authentic self to work has gained significant attention. Many individuals are seeking ways to foster deeper connections and achieve career success by showcasing their true identity in the workplace. However, striking the right balance between being authentic and maintaining professionalism can be a challenge.

In this chapter, we will delve into the importance of forming genuine connections, explore strategies for sharing your authentic self in a professional setting, and emphasize the significance of setting boundaries.

## Seeing Everyone as Human Beings

To truly share your authentic self at work, it is essential to shift your mindset and view every interaction as an opportunity to connect on a human level, rather than solely as a transaction. By recognizing the humanity in others, you open the door to building deeper relationships that can contribute to your growth and success.

Imagine you are attending a networking event where you typically view conversations as transactional opportunities. Instead, try to approach each interaction with a genuine curiosity about the person you are speaking with. Ask open-ended questions, actively listen, and seek common ground. By doing so, you transform the conversation into a more meaningful and authentic exchange.

## Nurturing Relationships

Building authentic connections requires nurturing relationships beyond the confines of professional needs. One powerful tool for achieving this is active listening. By genuinely paying attention to other people's interests and passions, you demonstrate your investment in their lives. This can be as simple as remembering a colleague's favorite hobby or following up on a conversation about their personal goals. These small gestures show that you value them as individuals beyond their professional contributions.

Suppose you have a colleague who is passionate about environmental sustainability. During a lunch break, they mention their involvement in a local nonprofit organization focused on conservation efforts. Following up on this conversation, you come across an article about renewable energy and forward it to your colleague with a note expressing your interest in their cause. This small gesture shows your genuine interest and strengthens your connection beyond the confines of work-related matters.

**Sustainable Authenticity**

While it is important to share your authentic self, it is equally crucial to set boundaries. Vulnerability should be reserved for those relationships that have proven deserving and trustworthy. Not everyone in the workplace needs to witness your vulnerability. Focus your energy on cultivating relationships that energize and inspire you, as these connections will provide the support and understanding necessary for your personal and professional growth.

As you become more comfortable sharing your authentic self, it is crucial to discern which relationships should receive a deeper level of vulnerability. For example, you may have a mentor or a close colleague who has consistently supported you and shown a genuine interest in your growth. These individuals have earned the privilege of seeing your vulnerability, as they provide a safe space for personal expression and offer valuable guidance.

**Conclusion**

Striking the balance between sharing your authentic self and maintaining professionalism is a delicate art. By adopting a mindset that sees everyone as human beings, nurturing relationships beyond professional needs, and setting boundaries, you can create a work environment that fosters genuine connections and personal growth. Remember, authenticity is a powerful tool that, when used wisely and sustainably, can propel your career to new heights.

# ACHIEVING YOUR FULL POTENTIAL

## ACHIEVING YOUR FULL POTENTIAL

# Chapter 30

## The Art of Building Trust: Strategies for Managing a Colleague Who Doesn't Like You

As a new manager, one of the most challenging situations you may encounter is having a direct report who holds negative feelings towards you. This can be a difficult and uncomfortable experience, especially when you're trying to establish yourself as a leader and build a positive working relationship with your team. However, it's important to remember that the problem may not always be with the other person. It could be due to your management style, a bias you're unaware of, or a combination of both.

In this chapter, we will explore ways to manage this situation effectively and build a foundation of trust with your colleague.

**Reflect and Check Your Biases**

Before you can attempt to resolve the issue with your colleague, it's essential to take a step back and reflect on your own behavior and biases. Ask yourself some tough questions:

- Am I unintentionally treating this colleague differently than others?

- Have I communicated effectively with them?

- Have I made any assumptions about them based on their background or personality?

- Have I given them enough opportunities to share their perspective?

It's possible that you may be unaware of biases or behaviors that are contributing to the negative feelings your colleague has towards you. By acknowledging and addressing these biases, you

## Have an Honest and Open Conversation

Once you've reflected and checked your biases, it's time to have an honest and open conversation with your colleague. Use the GROW coaching framework to level up and openly air your challenges in working with them, and hear their side of the story. This conversation should be a safe space for both of you to share your perspectives and concerns.

Here are some tips for having an effective conversation:

- Choose the right time and place for the conversation. Make sure you both have enough time to have a thorough discussion without interruptions.

- Start the conversation by expressing your concerns and challenges in a non-judgmental way.

- Listen actively and empathetically to your colleague's perspective.

- Avoid getting defensive or dismissive. Instead, focus on understanding their point of view.

- Work towards finding common ground and solutions that benefit both parties.

**Continue Your Efforts**

Having one conversation is just the beginning. Building trust and improving your working relationship with your colleague requires consistent effort and dedication. Here are some ways to continue building trust:

- Follow up on the conversation and check in regularly to see how things are going.

- Show appreciation and gratitude for their work and contributions to the team.

- Involve them in decision-making processes and seek their input.

- Offer support and guidance when needed.

- Celebrate their successes and achievements.

**Seek Feedback and Be Open to Change**

It's important to remember that building trust is a two-way street. It's not enough to just make an effort to change your behavior; you must also be open to feedback and willing to adjust your approach. Ask your colleague for feedback on your management style and how you can improve your working relationship. Be open to constructive criticism and use it as an opportunity to grow and improve.

## Conclusion

Managing a colleague who doesn't like you can be a challenging and uncomfortable experience, but it's also an opportunity for growth and improvement. By reflecting on your biases and behavior, having open and honest conversations, continuing your efforts to build trust, and seeking feedback, you can work towards creating a positive and inclusive work environment. Remember, building trust takes time and effort, but it's worth it in the long run.

ACHIEVING YOUR FULL POTENTIAL

# Chapter 31

## The Challenge of Working with Colleagues Who Aren't Self-Aware: Strategies for Success

In today's workplace, self-awareness is a crucial trait for individuals to have. It is the ability to understand one's strengths, weaknesses, and how one's behavior affects others. However, research suggests that only 10 to 15% of people are truly self-aware, leaving a staggering 85 to 90% of individuals who are not. This lack of self-awareness can lead to a range of negative consequences, including decreased job performance, career stagnation, and ineffective leadership.

In this chapter, we will explore the challenges of working with unself-aware colleagues and provide practical strategies for dealing with them.

## The Consequences of Unself-Awareness in the Workplace

The consequences of unself-awareness in the workplace can be severe and far-reaching. Unself-aware colleagues may struggle to understand their own strengths and weaknesses, leading to poor performance and missed opportunities for growth. Without self-awareness, individuals may not understand the areas they need to improve, making it difficult to advance in their careers. Unself-aware leaders may struggle to inspire and motivate their teams, leading to decreased productivity and high turnover rates. Additionally, working with unself-aware colleagues can be frustrating and stressful, leading to decreased motivation and job satisfaction.

Below are some of the consequences of unself-awareness in the workplace and how it can impact job performance, career advancement, leadership effectiveness, and overall well-being.

a. *Decreased Job Performance*: Unself-aware colleagues may struggle to understand their own strengths and weaknesses, leading to poor performance and missed opportunities for growth.

b. *Career Stagnation*: Without self-awareness, individuals may not understand the areas they need to improve, making it difficult to advance in their careers.

c. *Ineffective Leadership*: Unself-aware leaders may struggle to inspire and motivate their teams, leading to decreased productivity and high turnover rates.

d. *Increased Stress and Decreased Motivation*: Working with unself-aware colleagues can be frustrating and stressful, leading to decreased motivation and job satisfaction.

## Strategies for Dealing with Unself-Aware Colleagues

Dealing with unself-aware colleagues can be challenging, but there are steps you can take to address the issue effectively. First, it's essential to communicate openly and honestly with unself-aware colleagues, providing them with feedback on their behavior and its impact on others. When providing feedback, use specific examples to illustrate the behavior or action that needs improvement. It's also important to focus on the behavior or action, rather than attacking the person's personality. Additionally, encouraging self-reflection and seeking support from other colleagues can be helpful strategies. If necessary, set boundaries and consider a change in leadership if the behavior is negatively impacting the team.

**Below are some specific strategies practical tips for dealing with unself-aware colleagues.**

a. *Communicate Openly and Honestly*: It's essential to communicate openly and honestly with unself-aware colleagues, providing them with feedback on their behavior and its impact on others.

b. *Use Specific Examples*: When providing feedback, use specific examples to illustrate the behavior or action that needs improvement. This helps the individual understand the issue more clearly and can reduce defensiveness.

c. *Focus on Behavior, Not Personality*: It's essential to focus on the behavior or action that needs improvement, rather than attacking the person's personality. This helps to avoid hurt feelings and promotes a more constructive conversation.

d. *Encourage Self-Reflection*: Encourage unself-aware colleagues to engage in self-reflection, such as keeping a journal or seeking feedback from others. This can help them gain insight into their behavior and its impact on others.

e. *Seek Support from Other Colleagues*: If dealing with an unself-aware colleague is proving challenging, seek support from other colleagues who may have experienced similar issues.

f. *Set Boundaries*: If an unself-aware colleague's behavior is negatively impacting your work or well-being, it's essential to set clear boundaries and communicate them openly.

g. *Consider a Change in Leadership*: If an unself-aware colleague is in a leadership position and their lack of self-awareness is negatively impacting the team, it may be necessary to consider a change in leadership.

## Helping Unself-Aware Colleagues See Themselves More Clearly

Helping unself-aware colleagues gain greater self-awareness and improve their performance requires a proactive and supportive approach. One effective strategy is to encourage them to participate in 360-degree feedback, which can provide them with a more well-rounded understanding of their behavior and its impact on others. Additionally, offering coaching or mentoring can help them develop greater self-awareness and improve their performance. Training and development programs that focus on self-awareness, communication, and leadership skills can also be helpful. Furthermore, encouraging self-reflection and journaling can provide unself-aware colleagues with an opportunity to gain insight into their behavior and its impact on others.

Below are some strategies and practical tips for helping unself-aware colleagues develop greater self-awareness and improve their performance.

a. *360-Degree Feedback*: Encourage unself-aware colleagues to participate in 360-degree feedback, which can provide them with a more well-rounded understanding of their behavior and its impact on others.

b. *Coaching or Mentoring*: Offer coaching or mentoring to unself-aware colleagues to help them develop greater self-awareness and improve their performance.

c. *Training and Development Programs*: Encourage unself-aware colleagues to participate in training and development programs that focus on self-awareness, communication, and leadership skills.

d. *Encourage Self-Reflection and Journaling*: Encourage unself-aware colleagues to engage in self-reflection and journaling to help them gain insight into their behavior and its impact on others.

## Conclusion

Working with unself-aware colleagues can be challenging, but it's not impossible. By using the strategies outlined above, you can help them see themselves more clearly and improve their performance. Remember that everyone has blind spots, and it's important to approach these situations with empathy and understanding.

It's also important to remember that you can't change others, but you can change how you react to them. If an unself-aware colleague is negatively impacting your work or well-being, it may be necessary to set boundaries or seek support from other colleagues or a supervisor.

Ultimately, dealing with unself-aware colleagues requires patience, empathy, and effective communication. By using the strategies outlined above, you can help create a more positive and productive work environment for everyone.

# ACHIEVING YOUR FULL POTENTIAL

# ACHIEVING YOUR FULL POTENTIAL

# ACHIEVING YOUR FULL POTENTIAL

# Part 7

# Learning Teams and Organizations

ACHIEVING YOUR FULL POTENTIAL

# Chapter 32

## Overcoming the Tyranny of the Urgent: Prioritizing What Really Matters

In today's fast-paced world, it's easy to get caught up in the constant barrage of tasks that demand our attention. Deadlines loom large, and it's tempting to prioritize the tasks with the shortest deadlines, regardless of their actual importance. However, this approach can lead to a never-ending cycle of putting out fires and neglecting the tasks that truly matter.

In this chapter, we will explore practical strategies for breaking free from the tyranny of the urgent and focusing on what truly matters. We'll examine the importance of scheduling important tasks, isolating their most critical elements, managing anxiety, reducing time spent on unimportant tasks, and paying attention to the big picture. By adopting these strategies, you'll be better equipped to prioritize your most important work and achieve success in both your personal and professional life.

**Schedule Important Tasks and Give Yourself Ample Time**

One of the main reasons we prioritize tasks with short deadlines is that we feel a sense of urgency to complete them. However, this approach can lead to constantly putting out fires and neglecting more important tasks. To avoid this trap, schedule important tasks and give yourself way more time than you'll probably need to complete them.

For instance, if you have a critical project that requires careful planning and execution, schedule it for a time when you have plenty of bandwidth. Don't wait until the last minute and try to cram it in between other tasks. By giving yourself ample time, you'll be able to approach the task with a clear mind, focus on its most critical elements, and avoid the stress that comes with tight deadlines.

## Isolate the Most Important Elements and Make Incremental Progress

Not all tasks are created equal. Within each task, there are often elements that are more critical than others. To make the most of your time, identify the most important elements of a task and focus on making incremental progress.

For example, if you're working on a marketing campaign, identify the most critical components, such as developing a compelling message, creating a strong call-to-action, and targeting the right audience. Break each component down into smaller, manageable tasks, and focus on making progress on each one. By doing so, you'll be able to make steady progress towards your goal without feeling overwhelmed.

## Anticipate and Manage Anxiety

One of the biggest obstacles to prioritizing important tasks is anxiety. We often feel a sense of dread when faced with a daunting task, and this anxiety can cause us to procrastinate or avoid it altogether. To overcome this hurdle, anticipate the feelings of anxiety that may surround working on more important tasks and prepare yourself to manage them.

One way to manage anxiety is to break the task down into smaller, less intimidating parts. By doing so, you'll be able to focus on one aspect at a time, rather than feeling overwhelmed by the entire task. Additionally, try to identify the root cause of your anxiety. Is it fear of failure? Fear of the unknown? Once you understand the source of your anxiety, you can develop strategies to address it head-on.

**Reduce Time Spent on Unimportant Tasks**

Unimportant tasks can consume a significant amount of our time and energy. To make the most of your time, identify tasks that don't contribute to your long-term goals and reduce the amount of time you spend on them.

For instance, if you find yourself constantly bogged down in email, consider implementing a zero inbox policy. This means that you'll only check email at specific times of the day, and you'll aim to respond to messages immediately or delete them if they're not relevant. By doing so, you'll be able to reduce the amount of time spent on email and focus on more important tasks.

**Pay Attention to the Big Picture**

In addition to reducing time spent on unimportant tasks, it's essential to make time for activities that help you see the big picture. This can include taking a break from your daily routine to travel, catch up with friends, or engage in time-tracking exercises. These activities can help you gain perspective and refocus on what truly matters. By taking a step back, you'll be able to evaluate your priorities and make sure you're allocating your time and energy effectively.

## Conclusion

Prioritizing your most important work is essential for achieving success in both your personal and professional life. By scheduling important tasks, isolating their most critical elements, managing anxiety, reducing time spent on unimportant tasks, and paying attention to the big picture, you'll be able to focus on what truly matters. Remember, it's not about getting everything done, but about getting the right things done. By adopting these strategies, you'll be able to prioritize your most important work and achieve your long-term goals.

# ACHIEVING YOUR FULL POTENTIAL

# Chapter 33

# The Importance of Balancing Task- and People-Focus in Leadership

Effective leadership is a delicate balance between focusing on tasks and focusing on people. While it's important for leaders to drive results and achieve goals, they must also prioritize building relationships, inspiring their team, developing others, and showing empathy. However, the irony is that a focus on tasks can often come at the expense of a focus on people, which can ultimately deter success.

In this chapter, we will explore the importance of balancing task- and people-focus in leadership and provide practical examples of how leaders can achieve this balance.

## The Dangers of Overemphasizing Task-Focus

Leaders who prioritize tasks over people often miss out on the opportunity to build strong relationships with their team members. This can lead to a lack of trust, low morale, and high turnover rates. When leaders are too focused on tasks, they may neglect to recognize their team's efforts, fail to provide necessary guidance and support, and overlook opportunities to develop their team's skills. This not only harms the team's productivity but also hinders the leader's ability to achieve their goals.

## The Benefits of Balancing Task- and People-Focus

On the other hand, leaders who strike a balance between task- and people-focus are more likely to achieve long-term success. By prioritizing both tasks and people, leaders can create a positive work environment that fosters collaboration, innovation, and productivity. When leaders take the time to build relationships with their team members, they can better understand their strengths, weaknesses, and motivations. This allows them to assign tasks that play to each team member's strengths, leading to better results and higher job satisfaction.

## Practical Examples of Balancing Task- and People-Focus

So, how can leaders balance their focus on tasks with their focus on people? Here are some practical examples:

a. *Be Present and Engaged:* Leaders who are present and engaged with their team members are more likely to build strong relationships and create a positive work environment. This means being available to answer questions, provide feedback, and offer guidance when needed. Leaders who are present and engaged also demonstrate that they value their team members' time and contributions.

b. *Prioritize Feedback and Recognition*: Providing regular feedback and recognition is an effective way to show team members that their efforts are valued and appreciated. Leaders who take the time to recognize their team's achievements and provide constructive feedback can boost morale and motivation. This doesn't have to be a time-consuming process; a simple "thank you" or acknowledgement can go a long way in making team members feel seen and heard.

c. *Empower Team Members*: Leaders who empower their team members to take ownership of their work and make decisions are more likely to build trust and confidence. By providing opportunities for team members to learn and grow, leaders can develop their skills and increase their engagement. This not only benefits the team but also allows leaders to focus on higher-level tasks and strategic planning.

d. *Take a People-First Approach*: Leaders who take a people-first approach prioritize their team members' well-being and personal development. This means considering the impact of their decisions on their team and being willing to adjust their approach when necessary. Leaders who prioritize their team's well-being create a positive work environment that fosters collaboration, creativity, and productivity.

## Conclusion

Balancing task- and people-focus is essential for effective leadership. While tasks are important for achieving goals and driving results, leaders must also prioritize building relationships, inspiring their team, developing others, and showing empathy. By being present and engaged, prioritizing feedback and recognition, empowering team members, and taking a people-first approach, leaders can create a positive work environment that fosters collaboration, innovation, and productivity. Remember, task-focus and achieving results are vital for success, but without a sufficient balance with people-focus, success will be limited at every level.

# ACHIEVING YOUR FULL POTENTIAL

# Chapter 34

## Building and Maintaining Organizational Trust: Avoidable Pitfalls and Proven Strategies

Trust is the foundation upon which any successful organization is built. It is the glue that holds teams together, fosters collaboration, and enables employees to work together towards a common goal. However, trust can be a delicate thing, and organizations must be mindful of the pitfalls that can erode it.

In this chapter, we will explore some of the common pitfalls that can destroy organizational trust and provide practical strategies for avoiding them.

## Lack of Transparency

Transparency is essential for building trust in any organization. When leaders are transparent, they demonstrate that they have nothing to hide, and employees feel more comfortable sharing their thoughts and ideas. On the other hand, a lack of transparency can create an environment of distrust and suspicion. Employees may feel that leaders are hiding something, and this can lead to a breakdown in communication and collaboration.

For example, Enron's lack of transparency in their financial dealings led to one of the biggest corporate scandals in history. The company's leadership engaged in fraudulent accounting practices, hiding debt and inflating profits. Employees were kept in the dark, and when the truth finally came to light, it led to the company's downfall and the loss of thousands of jobs.

## Poor Communication

Effective communication is critical for building trust in an organization. Leaders must communicate clearly and consistently with their employees, listening to their concerns and addressing them in a timely manner. Poor communication can lead to misunderstandings, confusion, and a lack of trust.

For example, the failure of the Ford Edsel is often attributed to poor communication. Ford's leadership did not effectively communicate the car's features and benefits to their dealerships, leading to a lack of understanding and enthusiasm for the product. As a result, the Edsel was a commercial failure, and Ford lost millions of dollars.

**Favoritism and Nepotism**

Favoritism and nepotism can quickly erode trust in an organization. When leaders play favorites or hire family members, it creates a perception of unfairness and can lead to resentment among employees. This can create a toxic work environment and undermine collaboration.

For example, the Hewlett-Packard board of directors was accused of favoritism and nepotism in the hiring of CEO Mark Hurd's friend and former colleague, Leo Apotheker. The decision was seen as a breach of corporate governance and led to a breakdown in trust among employees and shareholders. Hurd was eventually forced to resign, and Apotheker's tenure was short-lived.

## Dishonesty and Unethical Behavior

Dishonesty and unethical behavior can destroy trust in an organization quickly. Leaders must set the tone for ethical behavior and ensure that employees understand the importance of honesty and integrity. When leaders engage in unethical behavior, it can create a culture of distrust and undermine the organization's reputation.

For example, the Wells Fargo fake accounts scandal is a classic example of dishonesty and unethical behavior. Employees were encouraged to open millions of unauthorized bank and credit card accounts in customers' names without their knowledge or consent. The scandal led to a loss of trust among customers and employees, as well as billions of dollars in fines and legal fees.

## Lack of Accountability

Lack of accountability can create a culture of distrust in an organization. Leaders must hold themselves and their employees accountable for their actions and decisions. When leaders are not held accountable, it can create a perception of impunity and a lack of responsibility.

For example, the Volkswagen emissions scandal was a result of a lack of accountability. The company's leadership knew about the emissions cheating software but failed to take action. The scandal led to a loss of trust among customers and employees, as well as billions of dollars in fines and legal fees.

## Practical Steps that Leaders Can Take to Build and Maintain Trust

Here are some practical steps that leaders can take to build and maintain trust within an organization:

1. *Be transparent*: Leaders should be open and honest in their communication with employees. They should share information about the organization's goals, progress, and challenges, and be willing to listen to employee feedback and concerns.

2. *Lead by example*: Leaders should model the behavior they expect from their employees. They should demonstrate ethical behavior, accountability, and transparency in their own actions and decisions.

3. *Foster open communication*: Leaders should encourage open and honest communication throughout the organization. They should create channels for feedback and concerns, and ensure that employees feel comfortable speaking up without fear of retribution.

4. *Build relationships*: Leaders should take the time to get to know their employees and build relationships with them. This can help to establish trust and create a sense of community within the organization.

5. *Recognize and reward employees*: Leaders should recognize and reward employees for their contributions to the organization. This can help to build trust and reinforce positive behavior.

6. *Provide opportunities for growth and development*: Leaders should provide opportunities for employees to learn new skills and take on new challenges. This can help to build trust and increase employee engagement.

7. *Address conflicts and issues promptly*: Leaders should address conflicts and issues promptly and fairly. They should be willing to listen to all sides of an issue and make decisions that are in the best interest of the organization.

8. *Be accountable*: Leaders should be accountable for their actions and decisions. They should take responsibility for mistakes and be willing to admit when they are wrong.

9. *Celebrate successes*: Leaders should celebrate the successes of their employees and the organization as a whole. This can help to build trust and reinforce positive behavior.

10. *Solicit feedback*: Leaders should regularly solicit feedback from employees to understand their concerns and ideas for improvement. This can help to build trust and demonstrate that the leader is committed to continuous improvement.

By following these practical steps, leaders can build and maintain trust within their organizations, which can lead to increased collaboration, employee engagement, and ultimately, organizational success.

## Conclusion

Building and maintaining trust is crucial for an organization's success, as it fosters collaboration, communication, and teamwork towards common goals. Leaders must be aware of the pitfalls that can erode trust, such as lack of transparency, poor communication, favoritism, dishonesty, and lack of accountability, and take steps to avoid them. By prioritizing trust and creating a culture of transparency, effective communication, fairness, ethical behavior, and accountability, organizations can build a strong foundation for success and achieve their goals. Trust is a critical component of any successful organization, and leaders must be mindful of the factors that can erode it to create a culture of collaboration and success.

# ACHIEVING YOUR FULL POTENTIAL

# ACHIEVING YOUR FULL POTENTIAL

# Chapter 35

## The Neuroscience of Trust: How Managers Can Boost Engagement and Performance

In today's fast-paced and competitive business environment, employee engagement and retention have become critical concerns for organizations. While many managers have tried various strategies and perks to address these issues, the impact has been limited. However, recent advances in neuroscience have offered new insights into the factors that influence employee engagement and retention. One of the key factors is trust, which is closely linked to the brain chemical oxytocin.

In this chapter, we will explore the findings of Dr. Paul Zak, a pioneer in the field of neuroeconomics, who has developed a framework for creating a culture of trust and building a happier, more loyal, and more productive workforce.

**Recognize Excellence**

According to Zak, recognizing excellence is one of the most effective ways to stimulate oxytocin production and generate trust. When employees receive recognition for their work, it sends a signal to their brain that their efforts are valued and appreciated. This recognition can take various forms, such as public acknowledgment, rewards, or promotions. However, it's essential to ensure that the recognition is genuine and based on objective criteria to avoid creating a culture of favoritism.

As an example, Google's famous "Thank You" program allows employees to recognize and reward their colleagues for a job well done. This not only boosts morale but also fosters a sense of community and collaboration.

## Induce "Challenge Stress"

Zak's research also shows that inducing "challenge stress" can stimulate oxytocin production. Challenge stress occurs when employees are given tasks that are challenging but achievable. This type of stress triggers the release of oxytocin, which helps individuals to focus and collaborate with others to overcome obstacles.

As an example, IBM's "Extreme Blue" program pairs employees with mentors from different departments to work on high-priority projects. This not only provides employees with new skill-building opportunities but also fosters collaboration and innovation.

## Give People Discretion in How They Do Their Work

Giving employees discretion in how they do their work is another key factor in stimulating oxytocin production. When employees have the freedom to choose their work processes and approaches, they feel more engaged and motivated. This autonomy also encourages employees to take ownership of their work and promotes a sense of accountability.

As an example, GitHub's "Friday Hackathon" allows employees to work on any project they choose, as long as it's related to the company's mission. This not only fosters innovation but also gives employees a sense of control over their work.

## Enable Job Crafting

Job crafting refers to the process of redesigning jobs to provide employees with more autonomy, variety, and meaning. When employees have the opportunity to shape their jobs in this way, they are more likely to feel engaged and motivated.

As an example, Atlassian's "FedEx Day" allows employees to work on any project they want, as long as it's delivered within 24 hours. This not only fosters innovation but also gives employees a sense of ownership and control over their work.

## Share Information Broadly

Sharing information broadly within an organization is another key factor in building trust. When employees have access to information about the company's goals, strategies, and performance, they feel more connected and engaged. This transparency also promotes a sense of collaboration and teamwork.

As an example, at Google, employees have access to a wide range of information through the company's internal platform, "Google Docs." This platform allows employees to collaborate on documents, share information, and work together on projects.

**Intentionally Build Relationships**

Building relationships is a critical aspect of building trust. When employees feel connected to their colleagues and managers, they are more likely to feel engaged and motivated.

As an example, Zappos's famous "Zappos University" provides employees with a comprehensive onboarding program that includes social events, team-building activities, and training sessions. This not only fosters a sense of community but also helps employees to build relationships with their colleagues.

**Facilitate Whole-Person Growth**

Facilitating whole-person growth is another key factor in building trust. When employees feel that their personal and professional growth is supported, they are more likely to feel engaged and motivated. This can be achieved through training programs, mentorship opportunities, and flexible work arrangements that allow employees to balance their work and personal lives.

As an example, Google's "70/20/10" rule requires that employees spend 70% of their time on their primary job, 20% on related work, and 10% on unrelated work. This allows employees to explore new areas of interest and develop new skills, while still fulfilling their primary job responsibilities.

**Show Vulnerability**

Finally, showing vulnerability is an important factor in building trust. When leaders are willing to admit their own weaknesses and mistakes, it sends a signal to employees that it's okay to be vulnerable and take risks. This can help to foster a culture of innovation and collaboration.

As an example, Tony Hsieh, CEO of Zappos, has been open about his own struggles with depression and anxiety. By sharing his vulnerabilities, he has created a culture where employees feel comfortable opening up about their own struggles and seeking help when needed.

**Conclusion**

Building trust is a critical component of creating a positive and productive work culture. By implementing these eight management behaviors, managers can foster a culture of trust, engagement, and performance. While it may take time and effort to see results, the payoff can be significant in terms of increased employee retention, productivity, and overall success.

As Dr. Paul Zak concluded, "Trust is not a soft, fluffy concept. It's a hard-edged, quantifiable driver of performance." By prioritizing trust, managers can create a work environment that is not only more enjoyable but also more productive and successful.

ACHIEVING YOUR FULL POTENTIAL

# ACHIEVING YOUR FULL POTENTIAL

# ACHIEVING YOUR FULL POTENTIAL

# Part 8

# Effectiveness and Productivity

ACHIEVING YOUR FULL POTENTIAL

# Chapter 36

## Overcoming the Tyranny of the Urgent: Prioritizing What Really Matters

In today's fast-paced world, it's easy to get caught up in the constant barrage of tasks that demand our attention. Deadlines loom large, and it's tempting to prioritize the tasks with the shortest deadlines, regardless of their actual importance. However, this approach can lead to a never-ending cycle of putting out fires and neglecting the tasks that truly matter.

In this chapter, we will explore practical strategies for breaking free from the tyranny of the urgent and focusing on what truly matters. We'll examine the importance of scheduling important tasks, isolating their most critical elements, managing anxiety, reducing time spent on unimportant tasks, and paying attention to the big picture. By adopting these strategies, you'll be better equipped to prioritize your most important work and achieve success in both your personal and professional life.

## Schedule Important Tasks and Give Yourself Ample Time

One of the main reasons we prioritize tasks with short deadlines is that we feel a sense of urgency to complete them. However, this approach can lead to constantly putting out fires and neglecting more important tasks. To avoid this trap, schedule important tasks and give yourself way more time than you'll probably need to complete them.

For instance, if you have a critical project that requires careful planning and execution, schedule it for a time when you have plenty of bandwidth. Don't wait until the last minute and try to cram it in between other tasks. By giving yourself ample time, you'll be able to approach the task with a clear mind, focus on its most critical elements, and avoid the stress that comes with tight deadlines.

## Isolate the Most Important Elements and Make Incremental Progress

Not all tasks are created equal. Within each task, there are often elements that are more critical than others. To make the most of your time, identify the most important elements of a task and focus on making incremental progress.

For example, if you're working on a marketing campaign, identify the most critical components, such as developing a compelling message, creating a strong call-to-action, and targeting the right audience. Break each component down into smaller, manageable tasks, and focus on making progress on each one. By doing so, you'll be able to make steady progress towards your goal without feeling overwhelmed.

## Anticipate and Manage Anxiety

One of the biggest obstacles to prioritizing important tasks is anxiety. We often feel a sense of dread when faced with a daunting task, and this anxiety can cause us to procrastinate or avoid it altogether. To overcome this hurdle, anticipate the feelings of anxiety that may surround working on more important tasks and prepare yourself to manage them.

One way to manage anxiety is to break the task down into smaller, less intimidating parts. By doing so, you'll be able to focus on one aspect at a time, rather than feeling overwhelmed by the entire task. Additionally, try to identify the root cause of your anxiety. Is it fear of failure? Fear of the unknown? Once you understand the source of your anxiety, you can develop strategies to address it head-on.

**Reduce Time Spent on Unimportant Tasks**

Unimportant tasks can consume a significant amount of our time and energy. To make the most of your time, identify tasks that don't contribute to your long-term goals and reduce the amount of time you spend on them.

For instance, if you find yourself constantly bogged down in email, consider implementing a zero inbox policy. This means that you'll only check email at specific times of the day, and you'll aim to respond to messages immediately or delete them if they're not relevant. By doing so, you'll be able to reduce the amount of time spent on email and focus on more important tasks.

**Pay Attention to the Big Picture**

In addition to reducing time spent on unimportant tasks, it's essential to make time for activities that help you see the big picture. This can include taking a break from your daily routine to travel, catch up with friends, or engage in time-tracking exercises. These activities can help you gain perspective and refocus on what truly matters. By taking a step back, you'll be able to evaluate your priorities and make sure you're allocating your time and energy effectively.

**Conclusion**

Prioritizing your most important work is essential for achieving success in both your personal and professional life. By scheduling important tasks, isolating their most critical elements, managing anxiety, reducing time spent on unimportant tasks, and paying attention to the big picture, you'll be able to focus on what truly matters. Remember, it's not about getting everything done, but about getting the right things done. By adopting these strategies, you'll be able to prioritize your most important work and achieve your long-term goals.

# ACHIEVING YOUR FULL POTENTIAL

# Chapter 37

## 3 Ways to Better Understand Your Emotions

Understanding our emotions is a critical aspect of personal and professional growth. Emotions play a significant role in our decision-making processes, relationships, and overall well-being. However, many individuals struggle to fully comprehend and manage their emotions effectively.

In this chapter, we will explore three practical strategies to better understand your emotions, enabling you to navigate through life with greater self-awareness and emotional intelligence.

## Cultivate Self-Awareness

Self-awareness is the foundation of emotional intelligence. It involves recognizing and understanding your own emotions, thoughts, and behaviors. Here are three ways to cultivate self-awareness:

A. *Mindfulness Practice*: Engaging in mindfulness exercises allows you to observe your thoughts and emotions without judgment. By practicing mindfulness, you can develop a deeper understanding of your emotional states and patterns. For instance, taking a few minutes each day to focus on your breath and observe your thoughts can help you identify recurring emotions and triggers.

B. *Reflective Journaling*: Keeping a reflective journal provides an opportunity to explore and analyze your emotions. Set aside time each day to write about your experiences, thoughts, and feelings. Reflecting on these entries can help you identify patterns, understand the root causes of certain emotions, and gain insights into your emotional reactions.

C. *Seek Feedback*: Ask trusted friends, family members, or colleagues for feedback on how they perceive your emotions and behaviors in different situations. This external perspective can provide valuable insights into blind spots or areas where you may be misinterpreting your emotions. Be open to constructive criticism and use it as an opportunity to grow.

**Identify Emotional Triggers**

Understanding the triggers that elicit specific emotional responses is crucial for managing and regulating your emotions effectively. Here are three strategies to help you identify emotional triggers:

A. *Reflect on Past Experiences*: Think back to situations in which you experienced intense emotional reactions. What were the circumstances surrounding those events? Identifying patterns in these experiences can help you recognize common triggers that lead to certain emotions. For example, if public speaking consistently causes anxiety, you can explore strategies to address this trigger.

B. *Pay Attention to Physical Sensations*: Emotions often manifest as physical sensations in our bodies. Paying attention to these bodily cues can help you identify your emotional state. Notice how your body reacts in different situations – does your heart race when you feel stressed, or do you feel a pit in your stomach when you're anxious? By recognizing these physical sensations, you can become more attuned to your emotions.

C. *Keep a Trigger Log*: Maintain a trigger log where you record situations that provoke strong emotional reactions. Include details such as the context, people involved, and the specific emotions experienced. Over time, patterns may emerge that help you pinpoint recurring triggers. This log can serve as a valuable tool for self-reflection and understanding.

**Practice Emotional Regulation**

Once you have a better understanding of your emotions and the triggers that elicit them, it's essential to develop strategies to regulate and manage your emotional responses. Here are three techniques to practice emotional regulation:

A. *Deep Breathing*: When faced with intense emotions, taking slow, deep breaths can help calm your nervous system and reduce emotional reactivity. Focus on your breath, inhaling deeply through your nose and exhaling slowly through your mouth. This technique can help you regain control and approach situations with a calmer mindset.

B. *Cognitive Reframing*: Cognitive reframing involves shifting your perspective on a situation to alter your emotional response. Challenge negative or distorted thoughts by replacing them with more positive and realistic ones. For example, if you make a mistake at work and feel overwhelmed with self-criticism, reframe the situation by focusing on the opportunity for growth and learning.

C. *Engage in Self-Care*: Taking care of your physical and mental well-being is crucial for emotional regulation. Prioritize activities that promote relaxation and reduce stress, such as exercise, meditation, or engaging in hobbies. When you prioritize self-care, you are better equipped to handle challenging emotions and respond in a more balanced manner.

## Conclusion

Understanding our emotions is a lifelong journey that requires self-reflection, self-awareness, and the willingness to grow. By cultivating self-awareness, identifying emotional triggers, and practicing emotional regulation, you can develop a deeper understanding of your emotions and enhance your overall well-being. Remember, emotional intelligence is a skill that can be honed, leading to more meaningful relationships, effective decision-making, and personal growth. Embrace the opportunity to better understand your emotions and unlock your full potential.

ACHIEVING YOUR FULL POTENTIAL

# Chapter 38

## Giving Effective Feedback When You're Short on Time

In today's fast-paced work environment, time is a precious commodity. As leaders, it can often be challenging to find the time to provide effective feedback to our team members. However, giving timely and constructive feedback is crucial for their growth and development.

In this chapter, we will explore how we can best go about giving effective feedback when you're short on time and provide detailed examples to help leaders navigate this common challenge.

## The Importance of Feedback

Feedback plays a vital role in improving employee performance and fostering a culture of continuous learning. When delivered effectively, feedback helps employees understand their strengths, identify areas for improvement, and enhances their overall job satisfaction and engagement.

## Prioritize Key Messages

When time is limited, it is essential to prioritize the key messages you want to convey. Focus on providing feedback that is relevant to the employee's current goals or areas of improvement. For example, if an employee is struggling with time management, prioritize feedback that addresses this specific issue and provides actionable steps for improvement.

## Be Direct and Specific

In time-constrained situations, it is crucial to be direct and specific with your feedback. Avoid beating around the bush and get straight to the point. Use clear and concise language to convey your message effectively. For instance, instead of saying, "Your communication skills need improvement," say, "When presenting in team meetings, I noticed that you tend to speak too quickly, which can make it difficult for others to follow."

## Offer Solutions and Resources

To make feedback more impactful, provide employees with practical solutions and resources to address the areas they need to work on. This demonstrates your commitment to their growth and development. For example, if an employee is struggling with public speaking, recommend relevant training programs or suggest a mentor who can provide guidance.

## Utilize the Feedback Sandwich Method

The feedback sandwich method can be a useful approach when time is limited. Start by delivering positive feedback, then address the areas for improvement, and end with another positive comment or encouragement. This method ensures that constructive feedback is balanced with recognition, maintaining a supportive and motivating environment.

## Use Technology to Your Advantage

Leveraging technology can streamline the feedback process, especially when time is scarce. Utilize tools such as performance management software or feedback apps to provide quick and efficient feedback. These platforms often offer templates or prompts that can guide your feedback, saving you time while ensuring the message is clear and effective.

## Conclusion

Providing effective feedback when time is limited requires a strategic approach. Prioritizing key messages, being direct and specific, offering solutions and resources, utilizing the feedback sandwich method, and leveraging technology can all contribute to delivering impactful feedback in a time-efficient manner. Remember, feedback is a crucial tool for employee growth and development, so it is worth investing the time and effort to ensure it is delivered effectively. By implementing these strategies, leaders can foster a culture of continuous improvement and help their team members thrive.

# ACHIEVING YOUR FULL POTENTIAL

# ACHIEVING YOUR FULL POTENTIAL

# Chapter 39

## Building Stronger Relationships at Work: The Power of Effective Listening

In today's fast-paced business environment, building strong relationships with colleagues, clients, and partners is crucial for success. While many factors contribute to developing positive connections, one often-overlooked aspect is the way we listen to others. Research suggests that the way we listen can significantly impact how others perceive us and whether they choose to trust us.

In this chapter, we will explore the importance of effective listening in building stronger relationships at work and provide practical tips to improve your listening skills.

**The Importance of Listening in Building Trust**

Trust is the foundation of any successful relationship, and it's no different in a professional setting. When we listen actively and empathetically, we demonstrate that we value and respect the other person's thoughts and opinions. This helps to establish a sense of mutual trust, which is essential for collaboration and teamwork.

Studies have shown that the brain forms an initial impression of a person's intent within just 0.07 seconds of a conversation. This means that the way we listen can greatly impact how others perceive us and whether they choose to trust us. By actively listening, we can convey that we're engaged, interested, and committed to understanding the other person's perspective.

## Four Tips to Become a Better Listener

Becoming a better listener requires practice, but it's a skill that can be developed over time. Here are four tips to help you improve your listening skills:

a. *Give the Speaker Your Undivided Attention*: In today's world, distractions are everywhere. It's easy to get sidetracked by emails, phone notifications, or other colleagues. However, giving the speaker your undivided attention is crucial for effective listening. Make eye contact, put away your phone, and avoid multitasking. This shows that you value the other person's time and are committed to understanding their perspective.

b. *Use Active Listening Techniques*: Active listening involves more than just hearing the words being spoken. It requires interpreting body language, tone of voice, and other nonverbal cues. To become a better active listener, use techniques like paraphrasing, summarizing, and reflecting. Repeat back what you've heard to ensure understanding and show that you're actively engaging with the speaker.

c. *Avoid Interrupting*: Interrupting the speaker not only disrupts the flow of the conversation but also convey's that you're not interested in what they have to say. Instead, wait for the speaker to finish their thoughts before responding. Avoid finishing their sentences for them or jumping to conclusions. This shows that you value their input and are willing to take the time to understand their perspective.

d. *Practice Mindfulness*: Mindfulness is the practice of being present in the moment, without judgment. It can help you stay focused and avoid distractions. By practicing mindfulness, you can improve your ability to listen actively and respond thoughtfully. Try taking a few deep breaths before a conversation or meeting to help you stay centered and focused.

**Conclusion**

Effective listening is a crucial component of building stronger relationships at work. By actively listening to others, we demonstrate that we value and respect their thoughts and opinions, which helps establish trust and foster positive connections. By implementing the four tips outlined above, you can become a better listener and improve your relationships with colleagues, clients, and partners. Remember, building stronger relationships takes time and effort, but the benefits are well worth it. By prioritizing effective listening, you'll be better equipped to navigate challenges, collaborate effectively, and achieve success in your professional endeavors.

# ACHIEVING YOUR FULL POTENTIAL

ACHIEVING YOUR FULL POTENTIAL

# Chapter 40

## Unlocking Meaning and Purpose at Work: The Power of Curiosity

In today's hectic and ever-changing work environment, finding meaning and purpose in our professional lives can be a significant challenge. While many of us are driven by the desire to succeed and advance in our careers, success alone does not necessarily lead to a sense of fulfillment or purpose. In fact, research has shown that curiosity is a critical factor in unlocking meaning and purpose at work.

In this chapter, we will explore the concept of curiosity and its role in creating a fulfilling work experience. We will also examine four practical ways to cultivate curiosity and intentionally create meaning and purpose in our professional lives.

**Crafting Your Work**

Crafting your work involves approaching your job as a craftsman would approach their craft. It requires a mindset shift from simply doing a job to creating art. When you view your work as a craft, you take pride in every detail, and you're constantly looking for ways to improve and refine your skills. Craftsmanship is about more than just producing high-quality work; it's about pouring your heart and soul into every project, task, and interaction.

For example, a software developer who views their work as a craft takes the time to understand the customer's needs and preferences, and they continuously look for ways to improve the user experience. They take pride in writing clean and efficient code, and they collaborate with their colleagues to ensure that the final product meets the highest standards.

## Making Work a Craft

Making work a craft means approaching your job with a sense of creativity and passion. It involves looking for ways to innovate and improve processes, rather than simply following a predetermined formula. When you make work a craft, you're not just going through the motions; you're actively seeking ways to make a positive impact on your organization and its customers.

For example, a marketing professional who makes their work a craft continuously looks for new and creative ways to engage with customers and promote their company's products or services. They experiment with different channels and strategies, and they use data and feedback to refine their approach.

## Connecting Work to Service

Connecting work to service means recognizing that our work is not just about us, but about the impact we have on others. It involves understanding that our work is a means to an end, not an end in itself. When we connect our work to service, we're able to see the bigger picture and understand how our contributions make a difference in the lives of others.

For example, a nurse who connects their work to service understands that their job is not just about administering medication and treating illnesses, but about caring for and comforting patients. They take the time to listen to their patients' concerns and provide emotional support, knowing that their work has a profound impact on the patient's well-being and quality of life.

**Investing in Positive Relationships**

Investing in positive relationships means building strong, supportive connections with our colleagues and customers. It involves recognizing that our work is not a solo endeavor, but a team effort. When we invest in positive relationships, we create a sense of community and belonging, which can lead to increased job satisfaction and productivity.

For example, sales professional who invests in positive relationships takes the time to get to know their customers and understand their needs. They build trust and rapport, and they continuously look for ways to provide value beyond the sale. They also collaborate with their colleagues to ensure that the customer's experience is seamless and exceptional.

**Conclusion**

Curiosity is a powerful tool that can help us unlock meaning and purpose at work. By crafting our work, making work a craft, connecting work to service, and investing in positive relationships, we can create a fulfilling and meaningful work experience. These practices allow us to approach our work with intention and mindfulness, and they help us to see the significance behind our daily tasks and interactions. By adopting a curious mindset, we can transform our work from a mundane obligation into a source of purpose and fulfillment.

# ACHIEVING YOUR FULL POTENTIAL

# Chapter 41

## The Myth of Hard Work: Why Intelligence and Direction Matter as Much as Effort

The idea that hard work is the key to success has been drilled into our minds since childhood. We're told that if we put in the hours and effort, we'll achieve our goals and be successful. However, research suggests that this may not always be the case. In fact, simply working hard may not be enough to guarantee success, and could even lead to burnout and disappointment.

Instead, it's important to focus on working smart and making informed decisions about how we direct our efforts.

In this chapter, we will explore why hard work alone may not be enough, and provide practical tips for how to achieve success by working smarter, not harder.

**Explore, Then Exploit**

One of the biggest mistakes early-career professionals make is diving headfirst into their work without taking the time to explore their interests and strengths. It's important to remember that exploration is a crucial part of the career development process. Taking the time to explore different roles, industries, and tasks can help you identify what truly excites and motivates you. This information can then be used to inform your career choices and help you focus your efforts on the areas that are most likely to lead to success.

To make the most of your exploration phase, try the following tips:

- Take on a variety of tasks and projects to get a sense of what you enjoy and what you're good at.

- Seek out mentorship and guidance from experienced professionals in your industry.

- Attend networking events and conferences to learn about different career paths and opportunities.

- Keep an open mind and be willing to try new things.

Once you've explored your options, it's time to exploit your findings. Focus your efforts on the areas that align with your interests and strengths, and work to develop your skills in those areas. This will help you stand out in your field and increase your chances of success.

**Use the 80-20 Rule**

The Pareto principle, also known as the 80-20 rule, suggests that 80% of consequences come from 20% of causes. In other words, a small percentage of your efforts can lead to a disproportionately large percentage of your results. To apply this principle to your work, take a close look at your daily tasks and projects. Identify the 20% of tasks that have the biggest impact on your goals, and focus your efforts on those areas first.

Here's how to apply the 80-20 rule in your daily work:

- Start your day by working on the most important tasks that align with your goals.

- Prioritize tasks based on their potential impact, rather than their urgency.

- Eliminate or delegate tasks that don't contribute significantly to your goals.

- Use technology and automation to streamline repetitive tasks.

**Prioritize Systems Over Goals**

While goals are important, having systems in place to support your efforts is even more crucial. Successful people often have systems that help them achieve their goals with relatively less effort. By focusing on building good systems, you can create a framework for success that will help you achieve your goals more efficiently.

Here are some tips for building systems that support your success:

- Identify the habits and routines that support your goals.

- Create a schedule and stick to it.

- Set up systems for tracking progress and measuring success.

- Develop a support network of peers and mentors.

- Continuously evaluate and improve your systems.

**Conclusion**

Hard work is often seen as the key to success, but it's not always enough. To truly achieve our goals, we need to work smart and make informed decisions about how we direct our efforts. By exploring our interests and strengths, using the 80-20 rule, and prioritizing systems over goals, we can increase our chances of success and avoid burnout. Remember, success is not just about putting in the hours, it's about working intelligently and intentionally.

# ACHIEVING YOUR FULL POTENTIAL

# ACHIEVING YOUR FULL POTENTIAL

ACHIEVING YOUR FULL POTENTIAL

# Part 9

# Your Journey Continues

ACHIEVING YOUR FULL POTENTIAL

# Chapter 42

## Reflections on the Path Ahead: Maintaining Momentum Towards Your Vision

We've come to the end of our exploration into maximizing your potential at work through strategies across nine key dimensions: work-life balance and well-being, early career development, career navigation and improvement, expanding your career impact, change management and adaptability, personal leadership development, leading teams and organizations, effectiveness and productivity, and planning for your ongoing personal and professional growth. I hope the multi-dimensional framework and actionable insights provided have given you a refreshed mindset and tangible set of tools to flourish in your career aligned with your true self. As you reflect on taking the lessons from this book forward, consider the following points to maintain momentum towards achieving your vision.

**Staying Grounded in Purpose**

While external factors will continuously change, keeping yourself grounded in your core values and purpose will provide an anchor. Revisit the self-awareness exercises from Chapter 1 periodically to check you remain rooted in what fulfills and motivates you most. This will help navigate inevitable challenges ahead from a place of intrinsic motivation rather than external pressures. When confronted with difficult decisions, referring back to your "why" provides clear guidance. Staying true to your authentic motivators is key for sustaining energy on your path long-term.

## Embracing Continuous Learning

The world of work is evolving rapidly, so maintaining a growth mindset is crucial. Commit to continuously updating your skills and perspectives. Stay up-to-date with trends through reading, conferences, networking or further education. View learning as an exciting adventure rather than a chore. Maintaining curiosity keeps you engaged and marketable, while personal development enhances life satisfaction. Schedule time for learning as ardently as other responsibilities. Remember - you have much to gain by growing into your best self each day.

## Mastering Accountability

While this book provided a broad framework, growth depends on tailored actions. Use the various models, checklists and exercises to craft your unique plan, with specific, measurable and time-bound goals addressing all key dimensions. Share your plan with close ones so they can support and hold you accountable. Commit to daily reflection - what worked, what needs adjusting? Keep your ecosystem, schedule and environment optimized for success by regularly reviewing progress and making course corrections as needed. Success lies in accountability to your true vision, not rigid perfectionism, so embrace small wins and celebrate the journey.

## Overcoming Inertia

Taking action is often the biggest challenge. Start by choosing one or two high-impact areas from your customized plan and tackling them with renewed focus. Small daily steps add up over time. When facing resistance, break larger goals into bite-sized pieces by developing a system to help form habits. Use rewards and accountability to help push through inertia. Progress may not feel linear but persisting through setbacks differentiates those who achieve their potential. With committed application of new learnings, you have the power to make each subsequent attempt at improvement more effective than the last.

## Asking for Support

No one achieves their vision alone - leverage your community for ongoing encouragement and advice. Develop an accountability partner to brainstorm strategies, celebrate progress and problem-solve barriers together. Seek mentorship from those further along their path for valuable lessons learned. Offer help to others too, as teaching is a superb way to embed new concepts. Ask close friends and family to understand how they can best support your journey through both words and actions. Holistic success depends on the relationships nurturing your growth every step of the way.

## Revisiting Your Vision

As you evolve personally and professionally, be open to refining your vision. Periodically re-examine if it still energizes and inspires you - shift focus areas proactively rather than waiting for loss of passion. While developing expertise in one dimension, explore others to stay engaged and maximizing learning. Don't fear changes that enhance well-being or impact. Visualize a version of yourself one, three and five years down the line with gratitude for progress made so far, and renewed commitment to dreaming bigger. Achieving your potential is a lifelong journey of small improvements; with dedication and adaptability, limitless opportunities await you.

I hope this book has provided a solid foundation for living and working aligned with your authentic self and continuously progressing towards the vision that speaks deeply to your soul. But true success depends on sustained application through challenges and changes ahead. I wish you the very best taking these lessons forward with courage, compassion and perseverance. May your career and life journey be deeply fulfilling as you leverage your strengths each day to make a difference in your own way. Always remember - your potential has no bounds when guided by an inspired heart.

# ACHIEVING YOUR FULL POTENTIAL

# ABOUT THE AUTHOR

Jonathan H. Westover, Ph.D. is a 12X best-selling and award-winning author and podcaster, ranked # 1 HR, Innovation, and Future of Work industry thought leader (Thinkers360), ranked in the Top 30 in Management and Organizational Culture (Global Gurus), and ranked in the top 20 of global researchers in the following topic areas - "Future of Work," "Global Leadership," "Organizational Development, "Public Service Motivation," and "Social Impact" (Google Scholar). Additionally, ScholarGPS has ranked him the #18 scholar in the world for job satisfaction research. LeadersHum put him on their Power List of the Top 200 Biggest Voices in Leadership to watch. He is an entrepreneur, management consultant, teacher, and research academic based in Orem, Utah. He serves on a host of nonprofit, community, and association boards and committees and has received numerous awards for his teaching, research, and service to the community.

**Current Professional Roles**

*Academic*: Dr. Westover is a professor and chair of Organizational Leadership in the Woodbury School of Business at Utah Valley University, Academic Director of the UVU Center for Social Impact and the UVU SIMLab, Director of

Academic Service-Learning in the UVU Innovation Academy, and a Faculty Industry Impact Fellow in the Women in Business Impact Lab. He is Vice President and member of the Executive Committee of the Western Academy of Management, and he is an affiliate faculty member in UVU's Integrated Students, Master of Public Administration, and Master of Business Administration programs. Dr. Westover has been published widely in academic journals, books, and practitioner publications. He is a regular visiting faculty member in other international graduate business programs.

*Consulting*: Jonathan is an experienced organizational leadership, people management, and organizational development consultant and managing partner and principal at Human Capital Innovations. For two decades, he has worked to help transform organizations across the globe. He is also the producer and host of the Human Capital Leadership (HCI) Podcast and Managing Editor of the Human Capital Leadership Magazine. Previously, Jonathan was an external consultant with the firm Targeted Learning, and an internal consultant in the Human Resource Development office at Brigham Young University, in the corporate Organizational Development office at InterContinental Hotels, and in the corporate Organizational Development office at LG Electronics in Gumi, South Korea.

*Thought Leadership*: Jonathan is a member of the Forbes Coaches Council, a member of the Harvard Business Review Advisory Council, Non-Resident Fellow in Social and Development Policy with the Nkafu Policy Institute (part of the Denis & Lenora Foretia Foundation), member of the HR Certification Institute CEO Advisory Council and past member of the board of directors, member of the Humantelligence Scientific Advisory, Board Chair and Director of the Corporate Division of the Global Listening Centre, a CIPD Academic Fellow, and an Advance HE Senior Fellow. Jonathan has been published widely and quoted as a management expert in popular and professional media locally, nationally, and abroad (such as Forbes, The Economist, U.S. News and World Report, The Wall Street Journal, MSNBC, PBS, NBC, CBS, ABC, FOX, MarketWatch, HR.com, SHRM.org, HRCI.org, The Washington Post, and USA Today).

## Education

Jonathan received his Bachelor of Science degree in Sociology - Research and Analysis (with minors in management and Korean) from the College of Family, Home, and Social Sciences and his Master of Public Administration degree (emphases in Organizational Behavior and Human Resource Management) from the Marriott School of Management at Brigham Young University. He received his Ph.D. in Sociology (emphases in International Political Economy and Work and Organizations) from the College of Social and Behavioral Science at the University of Utah. He has also received graduate certificates in demography and higher education teaching from the University of Utah.

# ACHIEVING YOUR FULL POTENTIAL

www.ingramcontent.com/pod-product-compliance
Lightning Source LLC
Chambersburg PA
CBHW052139220526
45471CB00004B/1443